Existential Cognition

Existential Cognition

Computational Minds in the World

Ron McClamrock

The University of Chicago Press

Chicago and London

Ron McClamrock is associate professor in the Department of Philosophy and in the Department of Linguistics and Cognitive Science at the State University of New York, Albany.

The University of Chicago Press, Chicago 60637
The University of Chicago Press, Ltd., London

© 1995 by the University of Chicago
All rights reserved. Published 1995
Printed in the United States of America
04 03 02 01 00 99 98 97 96 95   5 4 3 2 1

ISBN (cloth): 0-226-55641-7

Library of Congress Cataloging-in-Publication Data

McClamrock, Ronald Albert
    Existential cognition : computational minds in the world / Ron McClamrock.
        p.   cm.
    Includes bibliographical references and index.
    ISBN 0-226-55641-7
    1. Philosophy of mind.   2. Philosophy and cognitive science.
    3. Knowledge, Theory of.   4. Existential phenomenology.
    5. Cognition—Philosophy.   I. Title.
    BD418.3.M36   1995
    128'.2—dc20   93-48967
                                                                                      CIP

⊗ The paper used in this publication meets the minimum requirements of the American National Standard for Information Sciences—Permanence of Paper for Printed Library Materials, ANSI Z39.48-1984.

CONTENTS

ACKNOWLEDGMENTS

O ver the course of writing this book, I've gotten a lot of feedback and helpful conversation out of the members of my intellectual community. For their comments on various parts of previous drafts, I'd like to thank Bill Wimsatt, David Walton, Mike Swain, Bill Sterner, Josef Stern, Lance Rips, J. P. Rosensweig, Chris Owens, Greg Mikkelson, Mitchell Marks, Jeff Honnold, Stuart Glennan, Dan Gilman, James Firby, Tim Converse, Rob Chametzky, Bill Bechtel, Irene Appelbaum, Phil Agre, and Marshall Abrams. For their contributions to this project through our conversations, I'd like to thank Paul Wilson, Kris Hammond, and Dan Gerler. This book really got started as a result of a seminar called "Epistemological Issues in Situated Computation" that I co-taught with Phil Agre at the University of Chicago in the Spring of 1990; thanks to the participants in that seminar—and especially to Phil—for spurring me to try to put together the views I found myself with in there. I'd also like to thank Kris and the gang at the University of Chicago AI Lab for welcoming me into the Lab activities and mostly humoring me when I whined about methodology too much. And thanks also to Credence Fogo and Jody Stoner for their help in typing and setting up the bibliography, and to the University of Chicago AI Lab for providing supplemental financial and technical facilities support.

Figure 9.1 is reproduced from Robert Leeper, "The Role of Motivation in Learning: A Study of the Phenomenon of Differential Motivational Control of the Utilization of Habits," *Journal of Genetic Psychology* 46 (1935): 41–75. Reprinted with permission of the Helen Dwight Reid Educational Foundation. Published by Heldref Publications, 1319 Eighteenth St., N.W., Washington, D.C. 20036-1802. Copyright © 1935. Figure 9.2 is reproduced from David Marr, *Vision*. Copyright © 1982 by W. H. Freeman and Company. Reprinted with permission.

INTRODUCTION

F or better or worse now, the paradigm has shifted; the notion of mind as information-processor moves ever-closer to the center of the conceptual web. But exactly how this general idea should be filled out remains open. This project is an extended argument for taking the information-processing view of mind in a particular way under the current state of the evidence (both philosophical and scientific): The mind—even when viewed as a kind of computational system—is an essentially embedded entity; one such that analyzing it in isolation from the environmental context in which it functions will be fundamentally misleading. The understanding of intelligence, thought, and action cannot "bracket off" the structure of the environment, but can only occur and be analyzed in interaction with it.

This idea of intrinsically embedded cognition has not been the conventional wisdom among those interested in thought as a (relatively) rational, intentional activity. Although the importance of the environment in the study of the structure of behavior has received significant attention from behaviorists, sociobiologists, and cognitive ethologists (not to mention philosophers of various stripes—e.g., Wittgensteinians and Existential Phenomenologists), the dominant thrust of the mainstream rationalist/empiricist tradition has been toward a consideration of the "inner" nature of mind. It's this tradition that contemporary work in cognitive science has largely picked up and carried into new domains,[1] and which is typically taken as accepted background by both advocates and attackers of the information-processing approach to mind. From Jerry Fodor's "methodological solipsism" to John Searle's "intrinsic intentionality," the idea that some *internalist* conception of mind underlies cognitive science is the dogma that's come to have its day.

---

1. See Gardner [1984] for a compelling account of the continuities here.

In fact, Searle, a critic of cognitivism, but *not* of its seeming commitment to internalism, puts the point as boldly as anyone: "Each of our beliefs must be possible for a being who is a brain in a vat because each of us is precisely a brain in a vat; the vat is a skull and the 'messages' coming in are coming in by way of impacts on the nervous system" [Searle 1983, p. 230]. But the connection here cuts the other way in this domain as well: Arguments have been offered against the methodological approach of information-processing psychology by arguing that human cognition does *not* honor such an internalist constraint. Dreyfus [1979] is perhaps the granddaddy of such arguments; but similar points have since been made by many [e.g., see Putnam 1984, Burge 1986].

I've mentioned three options: the cognitivistic conventional wisdom of internalism; the anti-cognitivism that accepts the internalist aspect of the conventional wisdom; and the anti-cognitivism that rejects cognitivism because of its apparent commitment to the false dogma of internalism. But all three of these are wrong, because they all accept the idea that information-processing accounts of mind must be internalistic. The rejection of that assumption is the most general theme of this book.

In what follows, I'll argue that successful information-processing explanation *isn't* (or at least *shouldn't be*) committed to internalism—that it should instead be committed to denying such a perspective. Anti-internalist arguments are then to be seen not as anti-cognitivist, but as supporting a particular clarification or transformation of the methodological outlook to be adopted in studying cognition as information-processing.

I'm certainly not alone here. There is now an emerging wave of thought emphasizing the degree to which mental activity is only analyzable in its interaction with its environment. From Tyler Burge to Perry and Barwise in the philosophy of language, to Herbert Simon's psychological and economic writing on bounded rationality, to the followers of both Marr and Gibson (as well as the emerging work on "purposive" and "animate" vision by Dana Ballard and his cohorts), to the emphasis on reactivity, improvisation, and enforcement in planning from Chapman to Dean, the word is spreading: *Interactivity* with the environment is no longer to be seen as the inconvenience it is for Cartesianism; it's to be embraced and exploited in order to get the psychological trains running on time—to reduce overhead, simplify representation, and dodge intractability.

Precursors

There are obviously philosophical precursors to the slant on an account of mind that I am advocating. It's not much of a stretch to see the tension here as one between a roughly Cartesian conception of mind, where the notions of belief, thought, goal, and mental process in general are taken as thoroughly internal—as in the sense of both Carnap and Fodor, *methodologically solipsist*—and a more naturalistic one, where at least some of the preconditions on mental activity have to do with the positioning of the thinker in some objective external world. Nor would it be too misleading to see the conflict here as similar to that between the "pure" phenomenology of Husserl—with its emphasis on the immanence and transparency to reflection of the intentional structure of thought—and the "existential" phenomenology that followed, including Heidegger and his emphasis on the fundamental status of "being-in-the-world," Sartre and his rejection of the "illusion of immanence," and Merleau-Ponty and his emphasis on the world as precondition on perception. Of course, the book's title comes from this parallel; and ties to phenomenological issues will be discussed explicitly in the final chapter.

For many, the allusion to themes from phenomenology has a foreboding scent about it. The isolation of the Anglo-American "analytic" tradition from continental phenomenology through this century has contributed to an alienation of issues even where none is appropriate; and the most notable entry of phenomenological ideas into the cognitive science discussion has been Dreyfus' wielding of the Heideggerian scepter in support of a very broad account of what computers can't do [Dreyfus 1979]. But in some ways, the basic conception of the project of phenomenology is as close to the "epistemic engineering" project of AI as any philosophy has to offer. Its central theme is the attempt to characterize the structure of thought in terms of a *task* or *content* structure for human activity (in the sense characterized in chap. 1) by elucidating something like the level of organization and description of the world in terms of which the world presents itself to thought. Thought and action are abstractly characterized in terms of their relationships to their objects, and at a level of organization where issues of rationality and goal-directedness arise.

Psychological precursors to this view are not hard to find either. I've already noted the connection to J. J. Gibson's "ecological" approach to vision. But the view is closer to that stated in the revisions and extensions of the Gibsonian outlook given by Ulrich Neisser, particularly starting with *Cognition and Reality* [Neisser 1976]. There he makes complaints similar to some that will occur throughout this book: He worries that experimental cognitive psychology's "basic assumptions go little further than the computer model to which it owes its existence. There is still no account of how people act in or interact with the ordinary world." [Neisser 1976, pp. 6–7] And the solution advocated is similar as well; he urges cognitive scientists to "make a greater effort to understand cognition as it occurs in the ordinary environment, and in the context of natural purposeful activity"; to make "a commitment to the study of variables which are ecologically important rather than those which are easily manageable"; and to "pay more attention to the details of the real world in which perceivers and thinkers live, and the fine structure of information which that world makes available to them" [Neisser 1976, pp. 7–8]. Neisser puts the most general point here quite nicely: "Perception and cognition are usually not just operations in the head, but transactions with the world" [Neisser 1976, p. 11]. Much of what follows will be a working out of just that theme.

Ontology and Epistemology, Task and Process

The characterizations of the world under which behavior is systematic with respect to it, the classes of phenomena in the world that get lumped together in the generation of human action—these are the ontology of the world that we must discover in order to explain behavior in it. The only way we have any idea how to make behavior systematic in the human world is to taxonomize it the way that the humans in it do—to find and resonate to that human ontology. To know what properties in the world we might try to get machines to respond to so that they will have a description that makes the world practically knowable, we need to find the characterizations of the world that allow mapping and explaining those behavioral systematicities in us. As far as we know, this is the only description of the environment that makes the problem of getting around the human world a vaguely tractable one.

One way to put a central suggestion here is that our epistemology must in the end be deeply dependent on our ontology. A theory of knowledge will in some sense require a theory of what's known; the working of knowledge will along the way need to say what this state *is*. Such an ontological account is roughly an account of the kind of world the agent is facing, what sorts of goals it has, and what kinds of opportunities for gaining information and taking action are available to it in that world. Tasks, on this view, must be defined not just in terms of, say, moving an arm (or even sending signals to the arm controller), but in terms of states of the world to be brought about—e.g., lifting food to your mouth. The focus will be first on the structure of actual knowledge and action itself, as opposed to the things that the knower must do in order to instantiate that knowledge.

This distinction between the account of the logic of the *task* faced in cognition and the logic of the *process* that underlies our abilities to accomplish the task faced will be a central one in the discussions that follow. As I'll bring out in chapter 3, I think this is the central idea in a variety of metatheoretical suggestions about the logic of cognitive explanation—including at least Marr's distinction between *computational* and *algorithmic/representational* theories [Marr 1982], Simon's distinction between *substantive* and *procedural* rationality [Simon 1981b], and at least one of the ways of taking Chomsky's competence/performance distinction [Chomsky 1965].

The Human and the Natural

In a way, cognitive science attempts to split the difference between the human sciences and the natural sciences. The idea is to move to some conception that you get from the natural sciences of giving tools for objectification or trying to get a certain kind of distance from your preconceptions about how the domain works. In the case of cognitive science at least part of the standard that's being set is something like the standard of *implementation*: that as a guiding principle, you ought to think that your theory should be in some very rough sense (and I'll come back to this) implementable, that you ought to be able to give something like an algorithm for generating the behavior.

On the other hand, cognitive science differs from the other sciences of complex organisms by trying not to distance itself too much from the level of something like goals, intentions, rationality and belief—as we would in doing the *physics* of an organism like you and me. It's an old and standard point that even if you understand every bit of the physics of a baseball game, if you don't know what an *out* is, and you don't know what bases are, and so on, you just won't be anywhere near understanding how baseball works. Shifting to an excessively fine-grained level of analysis of the complex activity misses important general facts, some of which govern the overall functioning and behavior of the system. I might know all the physics you like, but if I don't know what an "out" is, I'm not going to know when the baseball game ends—I have to be able to figure out when there are three outs in the bottom half of the ninth. With outs being tremendously *multiply realizable* and *context-dependent* phenomena [see chaps. 1 and 2], the physics just isn't helping here.

So cognitive science might be taken as a kind of attempt to smooth out the line between two positions: On the one hand, we try to keep the sense of a *human* science in that we give an account of human behavior at something roughly like the level of description that we might start with—rationality and goals. But at the same time, we bring to bear some of the same kinds of standards that we might have taken from the natural sciences. So we're trying to find some kind of middle ground. We take our own intentional human activity and put it in a kind of different framework; and in so doing, try to take at least one step back from it to objectify it for scientific study. We see it not as just taken-for-granted human activity, but as behavior that has to be accomplished by a certain kind of device.

What I Won't Do, and Why Not

One background assumption I'll make is that of starting from a roughly realist position about the relationship of mind and world. We are organisms that interact with an external world through our physical sensory and motor apparatus. This is not to assume that the properties of the world are to be seen as entirely independent of our relationship to that world. There are lots of ways in which I think that kind of strong "metaphysical realism" [see Putnam 1981] goes astray. Social properties of objects are in at least some sense partially constructed by us, and even more basic phenomenal properties—like the colors of objects—depend essentially on how perceptual systems like ours cut up the world. I believe that in the end, the naturalistic ties between our activity and our world push along the collapse of the traditional Cartesian dichotomy between mind and world. But that's an issue I'll put off until the last part of the book.

The account of mind I'll sketch here is also thoroughly within a generally materialist framework. I won't be arguing about the possibility of some kind of strong Cartesian dualism. There are, I suppose, two straightforward (and closely linked) reasons for this. One is that I find the standard arguments against dualism from something like the impossibility of interaction to be compelling; the other is that I take the bare assumption of materialism—taken as something roughly like Davidson's anomalous monism—to be a very minimal constraint on an account of mind. It entails no interestingly strong sense of reducibility, predictability, or redundancy for our mental lives. Some of this latter point will be given further support in what follows—especially in parts 1 and 4.

I also won't be dealing directly with any of what John Haugeland [1980] refers to as *hollow shell* arguments against AI. In contrast to a *poor substitute* argument (which "denies that (mere) semantic engines are capable even of acting as if they understood" [Haugeland 1980]), a hollow shell argument claims that "no matter how well a [machine] acts *as if* it understands, etc., it can't *really* understand anything, because it isn't (or hasn't got) X (for some X) . . . " [ibid., p. 32]. Although I will touch on a couple of well-known anti-AI arguments that are clearly of this class—Searle's "intrinsic intentionality" claims (in chap. 10) and Nagel's "point of view" argument (in chap. 11)—I will do so in each case for slightly different reasons.

As for the "hollow shell" strategy itself, I have my hesitations. Philip Kitcher [Kitcher 1985] has suggested that what a progression like Darwin's really offered was a form of explanation for a set of phenomena which previously weren't even in realm of naturalistic explanation. "Why are those organisms like that?" wasn't a question for which we *could* have had an explanation; it was simply God's plan. But by putting it into that realm, he started the naturalistic explanation of some phenomena which led in the end to a kind of rejection of biological vitalism. But without anything like "Darwin's achievement" in the study of the mind that might bring the subjective character of experience into the realm of the explainable, we will fail to meet a prerequisite for making any reasonable judgement about "mental vitalism." Perhaps theory construction down paths that are now opening up will put us in a position to make better informed judgements about this kind of "mental vitalism." But without a more detailed account as to how the "how is it *possible*?" story of subjectivity gets cashed out, these anti-AI considerations are nothing but the deliverances of blind intuition-pumping.

Finally, with the flurry of discussion about the role of connection-ist models of mind relative to more standard AI models, I almost feel like I have to explain why this book isn't at all about connec-tionism. However, there are ways in which I think the discussion here will bear on the debate about connectionism. I will argue in part against the idea that the systematicity of intelligent behavior exists at either the level of classical AI structures *or* connectionist ones, but that it is a feature of agent/environment systems. The important contrast for me will be *local* (to the organism) system-aticity vs. interactive or embedded systematicity; and I'll argue that local systematicity doesn't do the job. But this claim is indifferent to how that level of systematicity gets represented or implemented in the system—connectionist, classical, whatever. So in most ways, my conclusions will be agnostic on the connectionist / classical AI debate. In some ways, though, the connectionists might get a bit of a victory here. The classical account (in isolation) doesn't give the appropriate systematicity on the current account, so the classi-cal support from systematicity [see Fodor and Pylyshyn 1988] is, perhaps, weakened.

But none of what I'll say in the following should be taken as implying that I don't think there are internal representations over which processes might be defined. I am not a behaviorist.[2] I think that the turn toward information-processing and internal represen-tation is an important and valuable one; it's just that it often comes with a denial of the importance of the cognitive systems' embed-ding in the environment. By refocusing so as to see both internal information-processing and interactions with the world as critical in the metatheory of cognition, we can take advantage of the strengths of each. Combinatorial systematicity comes naturally from a syn-tactic information-processor; but a detailed fit between specialized skills and the environment is more naturally seen as an interactive process. The details of how to go each way will be left until later, and on balance I will be arguing more for taking seriously the inter-active approach. But this is in part a sociological artifact, due to the fact that the current work (and particularly that by philosophers)

---

2. The shared anti-representationalism of connectionism and behaviorism is only one aspect of their similarities. I think they share many of their strengths and weaknesses (e.g., both seem plausible when focusing on automatic stimulus-response functions, but less so when we consider the more combinatorial, systematic side of psychological processes).

in cognitive science has largely been dominated by the internalist/representationalist bias.

Overview of the Book

The book has four parts which correspond roughly to four questions: (1) How would taking cognition as essentially embedded mesh with some general principles about scientific explanation? (2) Why should we be unhappy with the internalist status quo? (3) What does the embedded alternative have to recommend it? (4) What consequences result if we do accept it?

I. Intertheoretic Considerations. This part focuses on issues in the more general philosophy of science—about how "higher-level" theories and informational conceptions of complex systems fit into a more general account of scientific explanation and understanding, and how that fit allows for the possibility of a thoroughly "embedded" conception of mind. Particular attention is given to both a detailed view of levels of organization in complex systems, and the importance of the notion of *context-dependence* in explanation and taxonomy in the sciences. I'll suggest that a fairly strong notion of the autonomy of explanations at various levels of organization is the best account going of the relationship between the sciences. I'll also argue that *context-dependence* in the taxonomies of the higher-level sciences is acceptable and even the norm, and that this bears on the issue of *methodological solipsism* and *methodological individualism*. And I'll suggest a strategy for determining the answer to questions about "preferred" levels of explanation.

II. Bounding and Embedding. This part moves the discussion to the domain of information-processing explanation of complex behavior. Here, I synthesize a set of concerns about the possibility of Artificial Intelligence in particular (centering around the "frame" problem and issues of "bounded" rationality) into a unified problem for non-embedded accounts. I suggest how this approach may provide a kind of schema for dealing with that problem by facilitating a turn away from the approximation of optimal rationality and the universalizability it implies, and toward greater dependence on implicitly exploiting the highly contingent regularities in the environment. And I then begin the process of filling out the general framework for how this exploitation of contingency might work.

III. Minds in the World. Here I'll try to fill out and defend this strategic schema by bringing out its fit with progress in other areas of the study of behavior. In this part of the book, I'll make the strategies for boundedness through interactivity and embeddedness more concrete, by looking at some more specific shifts in the contemporary study of intelligent behavior. In chapter 7, I'll look at issues concerning the possibility of *decomposing* an agent's information-processing structure. In doing this, I'll offer a view on decomposition and modularity which will use embeddedness to avoid some of the pitfalls of more standard accounts of modularity and decomposition. In chapter 8, I'll consider the role that issues of language and meaning might play in the current discussion—particularly those concerning the "new" or "causal" theory of reference and meaning. These contemporary trends in the philosophy of language comprise some of the most explicit shifting toward an embedded account of cognition. And in chapter 9, I'll turn to perception, and particularly to vision, and consider both the emergence of the "animate vision" paradigm in machine vision, and how our current perspective can help bring out what I take to be the important germ of truth in the view—most closely associated with the work of J. J. Gibson—that perception is in some sense "direct."

IV. Philosophical Implications. Finally, I'll turn back toward some more philosophical questions about the place of mind in the world, and suggest ways in which the views put forward so far might impact on these questions. In chapter 10, I'll look at the issue of *intentionality* and how an embedded conception of intentionality might help resolve some contemporary puzzles (e.g., the causal impotence of semantic properties of representation, the "symbol-grounding" problem, etc.). In chapter 11, I'll consider the issue of *subjectivity* and how the current perspective might be taken as neither *reductionist* or *eliminativist* nor fundamentally dualist, but instead might give an account of a kind of autonomy of the phenomenological conception of mind. And in the final chapter, I'll explore some of the connections between the current account and a kind of naturalistic version of the general perspective of existential phenomenology, and where this view might leave the notion of human consciousness in our current scientific perspective by "thrusting consciousness back into the world" [Sartre 1957, p. 105].

PART ONE

Intertheoretic Considerations

AUTONOMY AND IMPLEMENTATION

I n these first three chapters, I'll consider how some background issues in scientific explanation might set up the eventual account of cognition that I'll be presenting. I'll focus particularly on how "higher-level" theories and informational conceptions might fit into our scientific world-view, and especially on the importance of the notion of *context-dependence* in explanation and taxonomy in the sciences. I think that a fairly strong notion of the *autonomy* of explanations at various levels of organization is the best going account of the relationship between the sciences. I'm starting with the more general philosophy of science not so much because foundations must in general come first; but because there are issues about picking among levels of organization which will come up repeatedly in the discussion that follows.

So here in chapter 1, I'll look at some general issues that arise in considering complex systems as having multiple levels of organization, as well considering the idea of the *task/process* distinction—a distinction that will get significant use throughout the book—and the relationship between these two ways of cutting up complex systems. Then in chapter 2, I'll consider the role of *context-dependence* in scientific taxonomy and explanation, and use the *level-relativity* of context-dependence to illustrate what's wrong with assuming a kind of *methodological solipsism* or *methodological individualism*. And in chapter 3, I'll look at the more general question of picking "preferred" levels of explanation, offer a rough schema for doing this, and suggest how we might in turn be able to make sense of a certain kind of notion "distal" causation without rejecting a general materialist world-view.

1.1. Levels and Multiple Realizability

It has become a central tenet of the current conventional wisdom in the philosophy of science that complex systems are to be seen as typically having multiple levels of organization. The standard model of the multiple levels of a complex system is a rough hierarchy, with the components at each ascending level being some kind of composite made up of the entities present at the next level down. We thus often have explanations of a system's behavior at higher (coarser-grained) and lower (finer-grained) levels. The behavior of a complex system—a particular organism, say—might then be explained at various levels of organization, including (but not restricted to) ones that are biochemical, cellular, and psychological. And similarly, a given computer can be analyzed and its behavior explained by characterizing it in terms of the structure of its component logic gates, the machine language program it's running, the LISP or Pascal program it's running, the accounting task it's performing, and so on.

This is of course all taken as compatible with the basic (or as John Haugeland [1982] appropriately puts it, "vapid") materialism of the *generality of physics:* Fix the physics of the universe and you have fixed all of its properties and processes; no further "occult" properties determine the structure of the world.[1] From this perspective, lower-level explanations don't eliminate or contradict those at the higher level; they instead explain how those higher-level processes can take place in a physical system. Thus, a knowledge of the chemical nature of the processes involved in cell division does not conflict in any way with the more common cytological story; rather, it fills in its presuppositions.

The strengths of higher-level explanations are roughly of two sorts: One, the capturing of generalizations that would otherwise be missed; the other, the illumination and extension of lower-level analyses of the systems. Let me look briefly at each of these in turn.

Higher-level explanations allow us to explain as a natural class things with different underlying physical structures—that is, types that are *multiply realizable.*[2] Thus, we can explain generically how transistors, resistors, capacitors, and power sources interact to form a kind of amplifier independent of considerations about the various

---

1. Note that this is very different from claiming that if you fix all the physical properties of any particular thing, then you fix all *its* properties of whatever kind you like. This latter claim is "strong" or "local" supervenience, whereas the former one is "weak" or "global." The strengthening amounts to a rejection of the *context-dependence of higher-level properties,* and thus (for reasons I'll get to) strikes me as deeply wrong.

2. See, e.g., Fodor [1974] for a discussion of this central concept.

kinds of materials composing these parts, or account for the relatively independent assortment of genes at meiosis without concerning ourselves with the exact underlying chemical mechanisms. Similar points can be made for indefinitely many cases: how an adding machine works, an internal combustion engine, a four-chambered heart, and so on.

This strength of capturing generalizations has many aspects. One is of course that higher-level explanations typically allow for reasonable explanations and predictions on the basis of far different and often far less detailed information about the system. So, for example, we can predict the distribution of inherited traits of organisms via classical genetics without knowing anything about DNA, or predict the answer a given computer will give to an arithmetic problem while remaining ignorant of the electrical properties of semiconductors.

What's critical here is not so much the fact of whether a given higher-level phenomenon is *actually* implemented in the world in different physical ways. Rather, it's the *indifference* to the particularities of lower-level realization that's critical. To say that the higher level determination of process is *indifferent* to implementation is roughly to say that if the higher-level processes occurred, regardless of implementation, this would account for the behaviors under consideration. (I'll return to this issue in more detail in chap. 3.)

It's worth here noting the connection of the virtues of generality and the issue of *tractability* that was raised in the introduction and will be a central theme of part II. The virtue of less complex prediction raises the issue that higher-level properties are the properties in the world which beings like us must be attuned to and react to in order to make getting around the world a tractable project. If we had to calculate the trajectories of all the particles around us to decide where to get our food, we would die calculating. But we don't. We detect and use other, more abstract partitions and taxonomies of the complexity we face.

The ways in which higher-level accounts enrich the ways in which we can talk about *dysfunctions* of systems provides a particularly clear class of illustrations of the virtues of such generality. Many dysfunctions of complex systems are really higher-level problems whose occurrence is entirely compatible with perfect functioning on the lower level.

To return to the computational case: There are many dysfunctions in computers that are simply not physical problems. A bug in a program is of course *somewhere* in the system physically stored, just like the rest of the program. But there is nothing *physically* wrong with such a machine—every transistor switches the way its input commands, every flip-flop changes state when triggered, and even every instruction the CPU gets is correctly followed. What's wrong with the system is not something physical, but something at a higher level of organization—at the more abstract functional level of the program.

Once seen, this idea of the level-relativity of dysfunction pops up all around. In the biological domain, true group selection can work by weeding out dysfunctions at the level of the group or colony that are not in any way dysfunctions at the level of the individuals that compose the group [see Sober 1984a]: In the case of the *myxoma* virus introduced to the rabbit population in Australia, the reduction in virulence of the viruses over time (in spite of selective effects for greater fecundity and virulence at the level of the single virus) is to be accounted for by the fact that overly virulent *groups* of viruses are dysfunctional, as they kill the host rabbit too quickly, thus reducing their chance to spread to other hosts through the primary vector for spread—mosquito bites. What goes wrong with groups of viruses here is a lack of fitness-enhancing behavior of groups, and not a lack on the part of individuals alone. A "dysfunction" (leading to the group's death) is occurring then in group level processes.

Other domains are not hard to find. In human social processes, dysfunction at the social level without a dysfunction at the individual level is the heart of the "prisoner's dilemma" and the "problem of the commons" in general rational choice theory. And the (too common, in my view) psychiatric suggestion that "all psychological problems are really chemical problems" shares the same problem: There may well be no particular facts about neurotransmitters, areas of cortical activity, or anything else at the physical level that are dysfunctional; but there still may well be functional problems statable at a more abstract level of description—for example, having very dysfunctional beliefs (e.g., that you're worthless), but for reasons that don't involve any brain dysfunction (e.g., because you were told this repeatedly by your parents as a child).

Any higher-level theory of a complex system will presuppose some background of normal functioning, or some notion of a "breakdown" case. The auto-mechanical account of my car is a perfectly good explanatory account of it. But heat the whole thing up to 1000°C and the theory is useless—maybe even just plain false. Similarly for computers with the power supply turned down to the point where "high" signals enter the "undefined" range in switching networks, and zillions of other examples I leave to your fertile imagination. But what counts as a breakdown, however, is clearly relative to the level of organization under consideration. A bug in your interpreter is a breakdown case from the perspective of explaining the machine as a LISP machine, but not from the point of view of explaining it as a complex of transistors: The program may not run, but the transistors just keep on switching; give them the right voltage in, and they give you the right one out. Similarly, focusing on the cognitive-level information-processing in a brain may well mean ruling out as breakdown cases situations where, for example, you have a .45 slug in your frontal lobe. But that would not be a breakdown case from the perspective of micro-physics.

1.2. Deciphering Lower-level Complexity

Let me move from the virtue of capturing generalizations to that of shedding light on the lower-level analysis of the system as well. The central point here is this: We quite typically need to know *what* a complex system is doing at a higher level in order to find out *how* at the lower level it accomplishes that task—that is, we often need to know the function of the complex system being analyzed to know what aspects of structure to look at.

The reasons for this are fairly clear. Not only is there typically a mass of detail at the lower levels that must be sorted through, but salience at the lower levels can be misleading, and can fail to pick out which lower-level properties are important to understanding the overall working of the complex system. So, to take a standard example: If you think that the heart is basically a noise-maker, the lower-level properties that will seem most significant might be things like the resonant frequency of the various chambers, or the transient noises created by the movement of the various valves. Or if you think of a computer as a radio signal emitter, you will see as most salient the high-frequency switching transients of the transistors and the exact frequency of clock signals, and basically ignore the difference between 0's and 1's represented by different DC voltages. Understanding the behavior of a complex system requires knowing which aspects of the complex mass of lower-level properties are significant in making a contribution to the overall behavior of the system; and this depends on having some sense of the higher-level functioning of the system.[3]

By looking at too fine a grain, or by trying to subsume *all* behavior under the more idealized account of systematicity (e.g., including cases where something in the system is just "broken"), we may well miss the particular behavioral systematicities that make, say, adding machines an interesting class of objects, and ones falling under an account which allows us to separate signal from noise (see above). If you were to focus on studying those that you've taken a sledgehammer to, you may be looking at exactly the breakdown cases for which the interesting properties and systematicities of the system have been destroyed.

This is of course not to say that systematic "errors" aren't really important: Our propensity to commit various kinds of fallacies in reasoning about probabilities (e.g., disregarding base rates, or over-assessing conjunctive probabilities) is an interesting and important bit of data about us as cognitive systems—part of the data that illuminate our use of a strategy of applying a "representativeness" heuristic for probability assessments, and thus data that shed important light on our use of general strategies in problem solving [see chap. 4]. Similarly, our "misrepresentation" of the relative lengths of the lines in the Müller-Lyre illusion may shed light on the use of an "interpret-as-3D" strategy in vision that leaves its mark without a conscious trace.

In short, understanding the behavior of a complex system requires knowing which aspects of the complex mass of lower-level properties are significant in making a contribution to the overall behavior of the system. And although it may turn out in particular cases that some measure of lower-level salience does correlate with higher-level significance, there is no guarantee whatsoever that this is always so. Determining overall significance and the sorting of noise from significant signal will thus, in the end, depend on having some sense of the higher-level functioning of the system. Trying to sort out which aspects of the lower-level activity of the system are significant and which are noise is a central aspect of what I'll call

---

3. Oatley [1980] gives a nice illustration of some of these points by discussing a thought-experiment where we imagine finding a typical microcomputer on trip to a distant planet and—not knowing what it is—apply various sorts of research techniques to it; the example does a nice job of illustrating some of the biases built into various methods and in particular brings out the importance of putting lower-level data into a higher-level framework.

a *distillation strategy*—an idea I'll return to several times throughout the book.

1.3. Task and Process

A somewhat different use of "level" that occurs particularly in the discussion of information-processing systems will also play a central role in the arguments that follow—especially those in parts II and III. I will refer to it as the distinction between *task* and *process*; but I take it to be the central idea underlying several well-known meta-theoretical distinctions, including at least Simon's [1981b] distinction between *substantive* and *procedural* rationality, Marr's [1982] distinction between *computational* and *algorithmic* theories, and Chomsky's [1965] distinction between theories of *competence* and *performance*.

Simon's notion is in some ways the most straightforward, and also has the advantage (at least in the current context) of being stated explicitly in terms of accounts of the rationality of systems. Roughly, substantive rationality is a matter of the fit between a system's goals and its environment; an account of it will characterize *what* the system *does* with respect to the environment. A system is substantively rational just in case it manages to act so as to achieve the satisfaction of its goals, as much as possible—although *how* it manages to do so is left open. And this is exactly the opening that an account of *procedural* rationality fills—an account of the *procedures* by which that process of fit actually works (to whatever extent it does). So whereas an account of substantive rationality will characterize adaptively "right" behavior for a system with particular goals in a particular environment, an account of that system's *procedural* rationality would instead characterize how it manages to implement and/or discover such appropriate adaptive behavior [Simon 1981a, p. 31].

For Marr, the *computational* theory of a device is (like Simon's notion of substantive rationality) an idealization about *what* the device does and *why*. It is likewise seen as independent from and in some ways prior to the theory of the underlying implementing processes, which Marr calls the level of *representation and algorithm*. *Computational theory* examines the goal of the computation, why it's appropriate, and the logic of the strategy by which it can be carried out [see Marr 1982, especially chap. 1.2]. In contrast, the account of *representation and algorithm* examines how this computational theory can be implemented by giving a representation for the input and output and an algorithm for the transformation [Marr 1982, p. 25].[4]

Perhaps the best-known (or at least most-mentioned) of these theoretical distinctions is Chomsky's competence/performance distinction. As it's put in perhaps his most central presentation of the distinction [Chomsky 1965, chap. 1], the central idea of a competence theory is that of an idealization about the systematic behavior of the organism under idealized circumstances. The competence theory of a domain of behavior (linguistic behavior in Chomsky's own case)[5] is seen as a formalization of the behavior via "a system of rules that in some explicit and well-defined way assigns structural descriptions to sentences . . . . It attempts to characterize in the most neutral possible terms the knowledge of the language that provides the basis for actual use of language by a speaker-hearer" [Chomsky 1965, pp. 8–9]. As with the other distinctions, the independence from considerations about actual production or performance is emphasized; it claims "nothing about how the speaker or hearer might proceed, in some practical or efficient way" [Chomsky 1965, p. 9].

The similarities between the accounts are clear: All make use of some notion of the explanatory role of an abstract and idealized specification of the behavior to be achieved; of the system "doing what it's for"; of the *task* to be handled by some process or processes. And in each case, this *task* account is seen as significantly underdetermining the related account of how that behavior is actually produced. A given task account is then seen as compatible with various procedural/algorithmic/performance accounts and even with various degrees to which the behavior of the system might approximate the idealized account. All also explicitly reject the suggestion that the appeal to such an abstract task structure should be taken as implying that these strategies must be in any way explicitly represented within the system. The claims about the task accounts are claims about idealized problem spaces, and not about the algorithms or representations used.

---

4. Marr also has a third "level" of analysis with which he's concerned: that of *hardware implementation*. See McClamrock [1991] for an account of why viewing these as *levels* rather than something like *perspectives on a given level* is problematic.

5. Chomsky does, however, explicitly allow for the use of competence idealizations in domains other than language: "One might, for example, consider the problem of how a person comes to acquire a certain concept of three-dimensional space, or an implicit 'theory of human action,' in similar terms" [1972, p. 73].

There is an aspect of the use of idealization that occurs particularly in Chomsky's variant of the task/process distinction (less so in Simon's, and still less in Marr's, I think) that should be distinguished from the basic task/process distinction between *what the system does* and *how it does it*. For at least Chomsky, there is an appeal to some kind of *optimality*, or what *would* happen under some "ideal" conditions of perfect information, no real-time constraints, and so on. Chomsky makes this appeal quite explicit; for him, competence theories are "concerned primarily with an ideal speaker-listener . . . who knows its language perfectly and is unaffected by such grammatically irrelevant conditions as memory limitations, distractions, shifts of attention and interest, and errors (random or characteristic) in applying his knowledge of the language in actual performance" [Chomsky 1965, p. 3]. And even for Simon, the substantive rationality is thought to capture something like an optimal fit or maximization between goals and the environment.

For the moment, I'll just note that the question of seeing "perfect information" or "ideal circumstances" as a standard for the task theory is an independent claim about task and process, and not a fundamental part of making the distinction. In chapter 5, I'll return to this point and suggest how this independence might pose problems for certain kinds of rationalist accounts of thought and action. But for now, I'll instead turn to a slightly different way of trying to constrain and guide the characterization of task accounts, particularly in the framework of complex systems with multiple levels of organization that I've discussed earlier in this chapter.

There's an important connection between the task/process distinction characterized above and the compositional notion of levels characterized earlier. We might naturally see the task/process distinction as in a certain respect more general, and see the earlier notion of levels as one way to specify guidelines for characterizing the appropriate task account.

For example, in analyzing a complex computer program, I might specify the task for a given subroutine by a formula that specifies its I/O function. I might of course go on to give a process account as well—an account of the representation and algorithm it uses to produce that I/O behavior. A critical determinant of why I would pick that particular task account of the subroutine is its fit with the description of the system at a higher level of organization. What I need to know about the subroutine's contribution to the functioning of the system at the next level of organization up is the function that it computes; the idealization of task typically plays the role of a primitive black box at the next level of organization up.

But it's often not at all clear that there is a next level up, or what it is. For example, what is the task for language? Is it to calculate all the grammatical sentences? What's the task of vision? Is it to calculate basically the orientations, all the surfaces in the environment?[6] Although seeing the task as embedded in a hierarchy of levels may help in picking it out, lacking a systematic higher-level framework to fill out may leave you floundering to find the appropriate task account.[7]

This tie between levels and tasks can fill in the role of higher-level theory in sorting out the details of lower-level implementation that was discussed earlier. Sorting significance from noise in lower-level activity is the central role of what I've called a *distillation strategy*. It's reasonable to see this critical role of "distillation" here as being played centrally by some kind of task account of the activity. The connection of higher-level structure to distillation might then be seen as dependent on the fact that higher-level structure is a critical (but not the only) guide to task structure.

This kind of prior role for a task account is a theme that both Chomsky and Marr put forth as a central motivation for their own task accounts (Chomsky's "competence" and Marr's "computational theory"). In Chomsky's words, "investigation of performance will proceed only so far as understanding of underlying competence permits" [Chomsky 1965, p. 10]. And similarly for Marr, who says that "an algorithm is likely to be understood more readily by understanding the nature of the problem being solved than by examining the mechanism (and the hardware) in which it is embodied" [Marr 1982, p. 27].

Sorting out the complexity will require both separating functional significance from noise, and deciding which aspects of the function of the system are to be seen as central, fundamental, or basic, and which are further elaborations, extra benefits from added kludges, or even accidental by-products. Finding such a strategy for distillation is unavoidable (even if we just resort to some assumption that some kind of lower-level saliency is what's critical). But

6. This particular case will came up in significantly more detail at the end of chapter 9.

7. This is a problem we will return to in chapter 5.

such assumptions will have critical consequences for explanation and modeling.

1.4. The Pitfall of Overidealization

One particularly significant pitfall encountered in idealization about task accounts is the problem of *overidealization*. Overidealization can lead to misguiding research strategies because of the criticality of top-down perspectives on research. For example, an account that sees higher-level behavior as being too close to some notion of *optimality* may only *misguide* research, by providing an unattainable and misleading goal or standard. Such a mistake will be a key focus of chapter 5.

Such errors of overidealization have occurred in the use of evolutionary explanations. The "panglossian" view of evolution and natural selection suggests that features of evolved systems should be assumed to be *functional*, and as having some kind of explanation for their presence available by appeal to the feature's contribution to the fitness of the organism. But the panglossian outlook has now largely been rejected, as the idea of accidental and indirect selection effects has become clear [see, e.g., Gould and Lewontin 1984]. Since phenotypes are not straightforward and unambiguous maps of the underlying genotype (because of the complex interactive effects of the various parts of the genome in producing the phenotypical properties of the organism [see Mayr 1984]), many of the features of selected organisms are by-products of structures that are directly selected for.

And in the economic domain, the idealization to rational and optimizing market agents (which underlies such basic generalizations as the connection between supply and demand) not only seems too far from real behavior to be predictive, but it may also fail to provide a framework of explanation that allows us to sort between what's significant for the purposes of economics and what's noise. After all, it may turn out [see Thurow 1983] that the generalizations of macroeconomics (which the rationalist micro-economic idealization is made in service of) hold largely in virtue of the facts about the market agents that this idealization explicitly leaves behind. The more those generalizations depend on microeconomic facts like the widespread use of price as an indicator of value, the more the idealization gives us exactly the *wrong* answer about what's relevant and what's noise.

1.5. Implementation and Context

The morals of non-reductive materialism have not been pushed quite far enough, in my view. One of the most critical things to notice is that there are cases where the relationship between the higher and lower level structures is not just *in principle* multiply realizable, or even in fact multiply realizable across different overall implementations of the higher-level phenomena. The degree of flexibility can be significantly stronger. There can be multiple realization of higher-level properties within the very same system; and even multiple realization of the very same token higher-level entity.

A particular case of multiple realization and higher-level generalization within a system worth noting is the implementation of higher-level primitives in computer programs, as it provides a particularly clear example of the possibilities of multiple realizability even *within* a particular complex system. Consider a particular variable in a program. At different moments in the running of the program, the machine-level implementation of the variable may be quite different. It will, of course, hold different values at different times; but furthermore, it will also reside at different real memory locations (as garbage collection may re-allocate variable memory) and so on [see, e.g., Wilson 1991]. What makes all those implementations of that variable an important and interesting class of things is that they play a fundamental and reliable role in the processes of the system at the higher level of organization. They may not share any terribly interesting properties at the machine level that they don't share with, say, implementations of other variables used in the system. And of course, as always, the way in which those variables are implemented on *different* machines will typically be even *less* likely to have anything other than their higher-level functional properties in common.

Of course, these sorts of phenomena are nearly ubiquitous in the social domains. An individual's wealth, a baseball team, a corporation, a story, are all cases where the identity of token and how it exactly implements the type over any significant time can vary dramatically in its properties at lower levels, and where the process of change and identity is determined by the rules of the game at the higher rather than the lower level of organization.

Notice that in this sort of example, there are really two factors that prevent the mapping: One is that multiple realizability allows different lower-level structures to implement the same higher-level feature; and the other is that *context-dependence* allows the very same lower-level structure to implement different higher-level objects in different contexts. If you pick the part of the system out on the basis of lower-level characterizations, the possibility that it is context-dependent features that are essential to the higher-level component means you still haven't necessarily picked out what implements the higher-level property. What will implement it may well change over time in the social and computational cases at least.

In fact, there's again even greater flexibility: It's not only that exactly the same properties of some local device might contribute differently to the overall functioning of a complex system—as when the same air flow control properties locally could be either functionally a choke or a throttle, and so on. But even more commonly, the interplay between levels and context-dependence will be of the sort where higher-level facts about context make the same local part play different functional roles *because they make different properties of that local part functionally salient.*

So, considering the example of the switching transistor: The weaker point is just that if the context is set up differently, the transistor switch might—still taken as a digital switch—represent different functions. But the stronger point is that varying context may make that transistor's switching into a different higher-level event, because the context forces different properties (lower-level properties) of the transistor to be the ones that are salient to the overall functioning of the system. Here, context determines what part of the mass of lower-level activity in the object is an implementation of some higher-level function *at all.*

It's time to turn to an examination of context-dependence.

CONTEXT,
TAXONOMY,
AND MECHANISM

T he need to place lower-level phenomena into a more global structure brings us to the phenomenon of *context-dependence*. To be a particular type of event or object often depends on occurring in the right context, and not just on the local and intrinsic properties of the particular event or object itself. So in the mundane realm, we can see that *being owned by me* is a property that my car has not in virtue of any local or intrinsic properties it now possesses, but in virtue of its historical and generally contextual properties of various kinds—the history of financial transactions, the referential and legal facts about the title deed for the car, and so on.

All this is relatively trivial. But it is perhaps slightly less so to note that this phenomenon of *context-dependence* occurs not only in the mundane social realm, but in the taxonomy of science as well—and particularly in the higher-level sciences. In this chapter, I'll show how bringing this out can play a key role in resisting what's been called an *individualistic* or *solipsistic* constraint on the methodology of cognitive science.

2.1. Context-Dependence

Examples of the phenomenon of context-dependence in the higher-level sciences abound:

- The position of a given DNA sequence with respect to the rest of the genetic material is critical to its status as a *gene*; type-identical DNA sequences at different loci can play different hereditary roles—be different genes, if you like. So for a particular DNA sequence to be, say, a brown-eye gene, it must be in an appropriate position on a particular chromosome. [See Mayr 1984.]

- For a given action of a computer's CPU, such as storing the contents of internal register A at the memory location whose address is contained in register X: Two instances of that very same action might, given different positions in a program, differ completely in terms of their functional properties at the higher level: At one place in a program, it might be "set the carry digit from the last addition", and at another, "add the new letter onto the current line of text".

- For mechanical systems—e.g., a carburetor: The functional properties of being a choke or being a throttle are context-dependent. The very same physically characterized air flow valve can be a choke in one context (i.e., when it occurs above the fuel jets) and a throttle in another (when it occurs below the jets). Whether a given valve is a choke or a throttle depends on its surrounding context.

So, chemically type-identical DNA sequences can differ in genetic role; physiologically type-identical organisms can differ in fitness and ecological role; structurally identical valves in a complex machine can play distinct functional roles; psychologically type-identical agents can have different social roles (as with the president and someone who thinks he's the president); and type-identical machine-level operations in a computer can differ greatly with respect to their computational properties. The context-dependence of many higher-level explanatory properties of parts of systems is thus a common phenomenon, and one that we should by now perhaps even expect to find in explanations given by the higher-level sciences. In such cases, the science in question may taxonomize objects with type-identical local physical microstructure differently—that is, the object's higher-level properties will not supervene only on its local microstructure.

In chapter 2 of *The Nature of Psychological Explanation* [Cummins 1983], Robert Cummins presents much the same idea in the form of the distinction between *interpretive* and *descriptive* specifications of sub-functions of a complex system. As he points out, a natural cleavage can be made between characterizations of a functional subsystem in terms of locally determined, intrinsic, descriptive properties of the subsystem, and characterizations in terms of properties that it has by virtue of the functional role it plays in the embedding system—properties that are globally determined, relational, and interpretive. As in the example above, a given action of a computer's central processor, such as loading an internal register with the contents of some specified memory location, might be specified intrinsically as, say, "load A with the contents of X." But that very same action might, given the program in which it is embedded, be specified as "get the next significant digit in the calculation"; or in another place in that program, "get the next letter on the current line of text." The very same descriptively characterized operation can be an instance of the former interpretively specified action in one instance and of the latter on some other occasion. Generally, a descriptive characterization of an operation or a subsystem specifies it in terms of properties that supervene on functionally or physically local properties. In contrast, an interpretive specification characterizes it in terms of its relationally specified, more literally "functional" properties—properties that needn't supervene on any particular localized proper subset of the properties of the overall system.

Cummins' discussion is an exception to a widespread bias in the philosophy of psychology (but not the philosophy of biology) of the last 20 years to make the non-reductive aspect of materialism captured by the notion of multiple realizability quite explicit, while at the same time more or less disregarding the role of context-dependence. But context-dependence is also a critical part of the question of inter-level relationships, as I'll be arguing in this chapter and the next.

None of this should be taken to suggest that any and all relational properties of objects and structures are necessarily legitimate parts of some scientific taxonomy at some level or another. Nature may still have distinct joints at which we must carve, and relational properties that are, roughly speaking, causally irrelevant are not going to be a part of any scientific taxonomy. The property of being a "fridgeon"—being a particle in a universe in which the light in my fridge is on [see Fodor 1987b]—will likely appear in no scientific explanations at all. Relatively stable causal mechanisms that are sensitive to particular properties may be central to including those properties in one's naturalized ontology. But those mechanisms at times may be defined over properties of objects and structures that are context-dependent.

2.2. The Level-relativity of Context-dependence

It's also important to see that considerations about context-dependence can and should arise at more than one level of analysis of a complex system, and may have quite different answers at the different levels; i.e., the lower-level events that determine the scientifically interesting properties of a structure can vary dramatically relative to the level of organization at which we are trying to capture the structure's functioning. For example, the properties of DNA sequences as objects of *chemistry* depend only on their local physical structure. But their properties as *genes* depend on their overall contribution to the phenotype; and what contribution they make to the phenotype is highly dependent on context—on where the sequence is in relation to the rest of the genetic materials, and on the precise nature of the coding mechanisms that act on the sequences. So the properties of a particular gene considered as that kind of DNA sequence are supervenient on its local microstructure, but its properties considered as that kind of *gene* are not.

The same point holds for the descriptive vs. interpretive distinction at more than one level of analysis of a system. So, for example, from the point of view of a LISP program, a function like (car(list)) (i.e., "get the first item on the list named 'list'") is a descriptive characterization of that action, whereas the correct interpretive characterization of that operation in a particular case might be "get the name of the student with the highest score on the midterm." But from the machine language point of view, the LISP characterization would be an interpretive analysis of some sequence of machine language instruction—a sequence of instructions that might play a different role in some other context.

In fact, for at least one level of application of the object/context or interpretive/descriptive distinction, it's plausible to see it as one way of making the distinction between syntactic and semantic properties of a representational system. The syntactic or formal properties of a representation are typically thought of as those the representation has in virtue of its shape, or if you like, its local structural properties. Relationships to other representations in the system that are inferentially linked to it or to the objects in the world it represents are not typically considered syntactic properties of the representation, but rather semantic ones. The significance of the representation for the system, its overall functional (or sometimes even "conceptual") role—these are the sorts of properties often thought of as bound up with the idea of the meaning rather than the form of the representation. These are also just the sorts of properties that lie at the heart of the interpretive side of the interpretive/descriptive distinction.

The critical point for present purposes is that these sorts of context-dependence make the answers to questions of localization *relative to ways of taxonomizing systems*. For DNA sequences to be type-identical as objects of *chemistry* is just for them to have the same (local) chemical structure; but to be type-identical taxonomized as *genes* is very roughly to make the same contribution to the phenotype. But since the contribution made to the phenotype is highly dependent on context—on where the sequence is in relation to the rest of the genetic materials, and on the precise nature of the coding mechanisms that act on the sequences—the canonical type of a particular gene *considered as that kind of DNA sequence* is supervenient on *just* its local microstructure, but its canonical type *considered as that kind of gene* is *not.*[1]

So an object's explanatorily relevant properties and on what they might supervene depend on the *kind* of thing we're taking it to be—on the level of organization and explanation we're considering. Viewing an object as a brown-eyed gene presupposes facts about its genetic role (which depend on more than local microstructure), while viewing it as DNA presupposes only facts about its chemical properties (which *do* depend *only* on local microstructure). So chemically type-identical DNA sequences can differ in genetic role; physiologically type-identical organisms can differ in fitness and ecological role; structurally identical valves in a complex machine can play entirely distinct functional roles (as with intake and exhaust valves in an internal combustion engine); psychologically identical agents can have different social roles (as with the president and someone who thinks he's the president); and type-identical machine-level operations in a computer can differ greatly with respect to their computational properties (as when, say, "store A at location X" is on one occasion storing the last digit of the sum just calculated, and on another is displaying the next letter on the screen).[2]

Overall: Higher-level explanatory functional properties across the sciences often exhibit context-dependence, so that the science in question may taxonomize objects with type-identical local physical microstructure differently. In such cases, the object's explanatorily

1. This is probably a slight oversimplification; there may be no unique genetic level of explanation. But for current purposes, this doesn't matter. Pick one such level above the chemical, and the point will stand.
2. These cases of might naturally be taken as illustrating the failure of a kind of parallel to what Fodor's [1980] *formality condition*—see below.

relevant properties *as that kind of higher-level entity* do not supervene on its local microstructure alone.

2.3. The Possibility of Non-individualism

That some general commitment to materialism—or even more generally to "non-occult" causation—should bring with it the assumption of some kind of methodological individualism has seemed remarkably obvious and trivial to some of the well-known advocates of this intimate connection. As Jon Elster says, "[the] view, often referred to as methodological individualism, is in my view trivially true" [Elster 1983, p. 13]. And with a similarly tautological tone, Jerry Fodor has claimed that "individualism is a completely general methodological principle of science; one which follows simply from the scientist's goal of causal explanation, and which, therefore, all scientific taxonomies must obey" [Fodor 1987b, pp. 42–43]. But whenever such a substantive claim rests primarily on the degree of obviousness claimed for it, our skeptical hackles should rise. This implication is not only non-obvious, but false. By making the appropriate explicit connections between the idea of *locality* and *levels of organization* in the higher-level sciences, we can make clear the fallacy in a particular kind of argument that is sometimes offered in support of an individualistic position in various domains.[3]

One broader goal here is to contribute toward transforming the general individualism vs. holism question from a largely metaphysical or even verbal dispute to a real, at least partially empirical question with a solution that avoids the triviality of simplistic reductionism ("only the little individuals matter") or the vapidity of complete ecumenicalism ("any level—individualistic or holistic—is as good as another"). By bringing out how the truth or falsity of individualism at a particular level of organization might be contingent on the facts about the particular structures occurring, it may help fill out how individualism *could* be false in given cases without implying any kind of non-mechanical or occult view of causation. It implies nothing more occult about causation than some facts about context-dependence and autonomy of level that are already a central part of entirely respectable sciences like genetics and computer science.

3. See Wimsatt [1984] on localization fallacies for a general precursor to this argument.

None of what I'll say questions the general metaphysical materialism that claims that if you fix the physics of the universe, you fix its higher-level properties as well. It just claims that this is entirely compatible with the possibility that lots of the interesting and perhaps even scientifically respectable properties of objects and structures in the universe are relational (e.g., teleological, informational, etc.) and non-individualistic.

The issue of *methodological solipsism* in the philosophy of mind and psychology has received enormous attention and discussion in the decade since the appearance of Jerry Fodor's "Methodological Solipsism" [Fodor 1980]. But most of this discussion has focused on the consideration of the now infamous "Twin Earth" type examples and the problems they present for Fodor's notion of "narrow content." Underlying this discussion are questions about the nature and plausibility of the claim that scientific explanation should observe a constraint of *methodological individualism*. My interest here lies in part in the role that a misuse of "methodological individualism" plays in Fodor's arguments about psychological taxonomy. But I also wish to use this as a kind of case study in examining the larger questions of individualism and *context-dependence* in scientific explanation.

Fodor's project in chapter 2 of *Psychosemantics* is largely to argue for the claim that psychological taxonomy ought to treat physically identical brain states as psychologically type-identical—that is, to argue that the states characterized by our psychological taxonomy "supervene on local neural structure" [Fodor 1987b, p. 44].[4] But why should we think that the causal powers of objects supervene on their local microstructure alone—as Fodor glosses it, that "if you're interested in causal explanation, it would be mad to distinguish between [physically type-identical] brain states"? [Fodor 1987b, p. 34]—i.e., that "you can't affect the causal powers of mental states without affecting the underlying physiology"? But before moving on to these questions explicitly, a small digression about *methodological solipsism* is in order.

Methodological solipsism is the claim is that taxonomizing psychological states via their contents (as given through opaque construals of propositional attitude ascriptions) is "give or take a little"

---

4. This is importantly stronger than what he (if not everyone) would call "methodological individualism"—the claim that psychological states are to be individuated *only* with respect to their *causal powers*.

compatible with taxonomizing them with respect to their *formal* properties; that "mental states are distinct in content only if they can be identified with relations to formally distinct representations" [Fodor 1980, p. 64]. And although it's not entirely clear what being *formal* amounts to here (Fodor admits that this notion will "have to remain intuitive and metaphoric"), this much is clear: Formal properties of mental representations are *local:* they are *internal* to the organism, and not dependent on relations to the external environment.

But as Putnam [1975, 1984] and Burge [1979a, 1982] (among others) have pointed out, examples of the effect of external context on the content of propositional attitudes are common. Whether one believes that they have arthritis, or that pans are made out of silver, depends at least in part on the social use of the associated terms in one's language, even if the socially ideal conditions for application of the terms have not been entirely internalized. Whether you believe you have arthritis depends on what "arthritis" means in your society's language, and that (via the linguistic division of labor) depends in part on what the experts say.

In acknowledging the point that there may well be *some* non-internal constraints on the content of opaque propositional attitude ascriptions—at least those brought out by the standard indexical and natural kind cases—Fodor qualifies his methodological solipsism. As he puts it, "barring caveats previously reviewed, it may be that mental states are distinct in content only if they are relations to formally distinct mental representations . . . *at least insofar as appeals to content figure in accounts of the mental causation of behavior"* [Fodor 1980, pp. 67–68; my emphasis].

The intent of this qualified formality condition is to claim that there is *some* kind of content ("narrow content") which *does* respect the formality condition, and which will provide the taxonomy of our "more mature" intentional (computational) psychology. The burden of finding some such notion of narrow content is an onerous one, however.[5] But importantly, the existence of narrow content depends critically on just the position that Fodor stakes out in chapter 2 of *Psychosemantics*, and the one that I will be questioning throughout what follows: the claim that whenever content differences *do* show up in differences of behavior, there must be a difference in

---

5. See Fodor [1987b, especially chaps. 3–4] for Fodor's own worries on this subject.

formal (and thus also in internal physical) state—that is, that psychological taxonomy ought to treat physically identical brain states as psychologically type identical. I'll now return to that claim.

2.4. Context and Causation

In fact, Fodor himself notes that there is at least *some* sense in which physically type-identical brain states might well have different causal powers: Say "get water" to Oscar here on Earth, and he will bring H_2O; make the same sounds to his twin on Twin Earth, and he will bring XYZ—i.e., the clear, odorless, relatively inert liquid that flows from the faucets of Twin Earth.

For our purposes, we should note that the differing causal consequences of physically type-identical brain states in different contexts will go far beyond this. Since on the wide notion of content, the contents of mental states are affected by social facts—e.g., what the experts believe—type identical brain states may often have different consequences in much more pervasive ways. Suppose Oscar and his twin both have mental states they would characterize by saying "I want to drive to Cleveland," but the route to the city called "Cleveland" is somewhat different on Twin Earth (although the difference has yet to show up in the Oscars' brains). Then their (initially) type-identical brain states will lead them to significantly different behaviors, as they progress through the use of maps, exit markers, and directions from service-station attendants. Of course, these differences in behavior are quite systematic. From here in Chicago, I can make a good prediction that Oscar will end up traveling east, even before he knows that, and in spite of the fact that his twin may well end up heading west (given the different respective locations of "Chicago" and "Cleveland" on Twin Earth). In fact, even their local behaviors might be identical—they might both intentionally head south on I-94 and take the third exit off to the right (labeled "Cleveland," of course). But none of these local similarities impugns the prediction about their eventual directions of travel.

This kind of systematicity and predictability in behavior would seem to underlie a significant part of the usefulness of real intentional accounts of action. Although the emphasis from rationalist-minded philosophers like Fodor is typically on the inferential and logical structure of propositional attitudes, a large part of the real force of propositional attitude ascriptions comes in explaining and anticipating actions *with respect to objects in the world*. Ascribing the desire to go to Cleveland to someone is useful at least partly in virtue of its regular connection with a particular object in the world—*Cleveland*.

Although I don't *need* it for present purposes, I intend to hold this non-internalist view in a *very* strong sense. It's not just that I think that there can be differences in the appropriate psychological classification of states of the organism in instances where the relationally characterized behavioral consequences differ but the locally individuated brain states don't differ *at any point in time*.[6] Rather, I think that physiologically type identical states should also count as different intentional states *because of their different but reliable tendencies to change in particular different ways as they interact with the structure of their embedding environment*.

So, for example, in the "Cleveland" case, I might have further restricted the example so as to keep the trajectories of the particles in their brains the same over time as much as possible, by making the same general turns, bodily motions, and so on. This kind of case is nice and clean, and makes the point logically strong. But I want to make the broader claim that even when the difference *will* eventually show up in the local physical properties of the thinker, the cases not only count as well as the "cleaner" ones but that in fact these are in the end the more central cases.[7]

In any case, there are then some at least prima facie reasons to see the systematic and predictive use of intentional explanation as depending in part on the subject's ability to take advantage of regularities in its world (including its *social* world) which it may not explicitly represent ahead of time. Or to put this in a slightly different way: The idealization about the organism which underlies an *intentional* characterization of its states may not only idealize on the basis of its current internal state, but also idealize about what *will* happen on the basis of those internal states, given the organism's ecological situation. So in some pretty interesting and systematic ways, it might seem that the causal powers (at least for the

6. This would be the kind of difference that's focused on in the standard kind of "Twin Earth" cases.

7. See chapter 6 for more on this.

purposes of *psychology*) of physically type-identical thoughts *can* differ.[8] But given the observations at the beginning of this chapter, perhaps that shouldn't be seen as particularly surprising: Issues of locality and context-dependence are relative to a way of taxonomizing the system, and it's a common occurrence (e.g., in the gene/DNA case) that explanatory taxonomies at different levels of organization will also give different answers to questions about context-dependence.

So the possibility of anti-individualism about psychological states is not an issue of occult causation; it's not ruled out by any "completely general methodological principle . . . which follows simply from the scientist's goal of causal explanation" [Fodor 1987b, p. 42]. The real issue about individualism is whether or not the taxonomic apparatus of psychology must presuppose facts about the embedding context in order to characterize the systematicity of behavior *at the appropriate level of organization or abstraction.* Of course there will be—at least in principle—accounts of human behavior that are solipsistic in nature: microphysical, chemical, and neurophysiological ones, at least. But these are a long way from an account of us as (fairly) systematically (relatively) intelligent and (sometimes) rational beings. The current point is that there may well also be scientifically respectable accounts that individuate the causally relevant states of the organism *non*-solipsistically. The prima facie inclinations to see intentional taxonomy as non-solipsistic *could* turn out to be overridden in the end; but they should not be overridden in the *beginning* by any putative "constitutive principle of scientific practice" of which I'm aware.

2.5. Fodor's Rebuttals

Fodor is not insensitive to the fact that there are at least some *prima facie* inclinations toward a relational account of psychological states. Feeling this tug, he offers two responses to the general suggestion. But the idea of level-relative context-dependence provides a clear answer to each.

Fodor's first rebuttal to context-dependent psychological states simply claims that on the view "that my mental state differs from

---

8. Fodor of course resists this sort of suggestion, claiming that its problem lies in the fact that "identity of causal power must be assessed *across* contexts, not *within* contexts" [1987b, p. 35]. But recall that *sameness of causal powers is relative to a way of taxonomizing a system.*

my Twin's, it's hard to see why it doesn't show that our brain states differ too . . . it would be grotesque to suppose that brain states that live on Twin Earth are ipso facto typologically distinct from brain states that live around here" [Fodor 1987b, pp. 37–38]. But from the current vantage point, it's not hard at all. The critical asymmetry between mental states and brain states may be essentially the same kind of level-relative context-dependence as we saw in the case of DNA sequences and genes. An object's causal powers and on what they supervene depend on the *kind* of thing we're taking it to be—on the level of organization and explanation we're considering. Genetic characterization presupposes facts about genetic role which depend on non-local properties, but analyzing the same object as a DNA structure will depend only on its local chemical structure.

Similarly, describing our brain states as *brain states* is describing them in terms of properties that presuppose only the local regularities of physical functioning; the causal relations presupposed do not presuppose facts about external context or external regularities. But to describe those very same states *as intentional states* may perfectly well be to describe them in terms of properties that *do* presuppose a context and external regularities, and thus may presuppose differences that do not supervene on the local physical structure. And considerations offered in the preceding section suggest that this possibility is in fact prima facie *plausible* for intentional states.

Fodor's second rebuttal (which he attributes to Ned Block) consists in presenting the following puzzle, which is taken to suggest the incoherence of taking an ecological property like *linguistic affiliation* as a determinant of individual differences—in this case, food preferences. Consider some psychologist interested in the etiology of the food preferences of Oscar (here) and his doppelgänger $Oscar_2$ (on Twin-Earth, where "brisket" refers to only *beef* brisket, for the usual contextual and social reasons). Now if we allow these social but non-internal facts to push us to a non-individualistic *psychological* taxonomy, then "Oscar and $Oscar_2$ have different food preferences; what Oscar prefers to gruel is brisket, and what $Oscar_2$ prefers is gruel to $brisket_2$ . . . ." The problem here is, he claims, that "then she has to say that there are *three* sources of variance: genetic endowment, early training, *and linguistic affiliation*. But surely it's *mad* to say that linguistic affiliation is per se a determinant of food preference; how *could* it be?" [Fodor 1987b, p. 40].

Here's how: Oscar might, for example have lots of linguistically mediated beliefs about "brisket" (e.g., thinks "Brisket is much healthier than other meats", "Brisket is more impressive to serve than other meats", "Brisket goes with the rest of this meal very well," etc.) which can play a critical role in his own food preferences. Roughly, if Oscar depends on things outside his head to determine what counts as "brisket" (as, via the linguistic division of labor, we all tend to do), *and* if some of what determines his preferences vis-à-vis "brisket" are beliefs about this general class (e.g., whether it's healthy, impressive, aesthetically compatible with something else, etc.), then linguistic affiliation may well be a part of his preference—it may, for example, help us predict what he's going to buy at the deli. The social use of the term "brisket" may be an important determinant in Oscar's behavior vis-à-vis various deli meats, just as the maps and exit markers were an important determinant of his systematically predictable driving-east behavior when he wanted to go to Cleveland.

This is not to say there is *no* sense to a solipsistic notion of, say, food preference—or for that matter, economic or political preferences. There are no doubt interesting and systematic facts about food preferences under circumstances where the subjects' information about the food in question is dramatically constrained in one way or another, and in particular where they are not allowed to take advantage of information that would be socially available but which they have not internally represented. Such facts about "preferences" are no doubt a legitimate part of psychology. But the relation between these facts and the notion of preference critical to normal intentional-level theorizing about human agents in the social context is far from straightforward. The normal ascription of desires and preferences to agents outside the laboratory is centrally to predict and explain their actions under normal informational conditions—not under artificially impoverished ones (as in the food tasting case, or perhaps the cases of tachistoscopic presentation of visual displays), nor for that matter under ideal conditions of "perfect information" (as with perfectly rational and well informed voters or market agents). It is an empirical matter whether or not real embedded preferences approximate either those of the circumstance of information impoverished so as to include only bare sensation, or that where information is idealized about and seen as perfect or complete in some way.

And furthermore, it seems to me that this is an empirical matter about which we're in a pretty good position to guess. Market agents and political agents typically work under conditions of dramatic informational (and cognitive resource) constraint; and their use of gross satisficing strategies (like using price as an indicator of value) leaves their behavior poorly modeled by an account of them as perfectly rational optimizers. Similarly, the influence of social factors on preferences may well leave them in practice a poor fit to the laboratory case of impoverished information. (If you've ever been in a blind beer tasting test, you know how you're as likely to choose Schlitz as Lowenbrau.)

It's possible that these considerations may leave some of the constrained-information preference data in much the same position as some kinds of mistaken stimulus-response generalizations. "Preferences" under conditions of dramatically constrained contextual information may be little more useful and respectable than behavioristic "responses" to linguistic items isolated from any kind of context. It is at least entirely possible that these kinds of "solipsistic" facts about "preferences" are another case—like that of behaviorism, or that of over-idealization in classical economic theory—where a methodology generated by mistaken epistemic or metaphysical views has been allowed to ride roughshod over critical facts about a domain.

2.6. External Mechanisms, Mental Causes

Fodor is, in my view, entirely correct in his insistence that "for one thing to affect the causal powers of another, there must be a mediating law or mechanism" [Fodor 1987b, p. 41]. Where he goes wrong is in his insistence that "the only mechanisms that can mediate environmental effects on the causal powers of mental states are neurological" [Fodor 1987b, p. 41]. Social and environmental mechanisms of all sorts may well mediate such difference in causal powers, just as the difference in the causal powers of type-identical DNA molecules at different loci is mediated by the external (to the genetic material) mechanisms of genetic coding, or as the difference in causal powers of type-identical organisms can be mediated by the different social mechanisms they may confront.

It's simply not the case that "if mind/brain supervenience goes, then the intelligibility of mental causation goes with it," because the causal powers of psychological states don't depend *only* on the underlying brain states either. But this is a long way from losing "the intelligibility of mental causation," because even if intelligibility of mental causation requires intelligible mechanisms, some of those mechanisms might well be partly out in the physical and social world rather than entirely within our individual heads. Maybe "God made the world such that the mechanisms by which environmental variables affect organic behavior run via their effects on the organism's nervous system" [Fodor 1987b, p. 40], but not *exclusively* so. And furthermore, *we* have made the social world so that there *would* be other mechanisms through which environmental variables might systematically affect human behavior.

One way to view the mistake that was made in the inference to individualism is as due to running together two distinct notions that might both be lumped under the general heading of looking for the essence, or the best description of some type of object. One question is taxonomic—or maybe, in a certain sense, *metaphysical:* What makes that thing one of those? What is it to be one of those? And the other is about structure, or composition: What are those things themselves like? What is its essential structure? In the genetic case, where we're looking for the "essence" of some particular gene or type of gene, an account of DNA structure might be a reasonable answer to the structural question, but not to the taxonomic one. The taxonomic question might instead be answered by giving some kind of characterization of the functional role of genes of that type.

Running these two sorts of questions together is the central theme in the idea of *localization fallacies* brought on by a kind of reductionistic bias. As Wimsatt points out, one of the central reductionistic heuristics for problem-solving is what he calls *modeling localization:* "Look for an intrasystematic mechanism rather than an intersystemic one to explain a systematic property, or if both are available, regard the former as 'more fundamental'" [Wimsatt 1986, p. 301]. The failures of this bias will resurface more than once in this book. But for now, let me just point out that the domain of intentional explanation—perhaps because the worries about "occult causes" are closer to the surface here—is one where the bias toward this strategy is radical among the individualists, to the point where the strategy of modeling localization is treated as though it followed directly from the denial of some kind of occult "social forces." [See, for example, Elster 1983, chap. 2.] And this is nowhere clearer than in the ascription of causal power to *contentful, semantic,* or *intentional* states. As Zenon Pylyshyn has put it, "the semantics of representations cannot literally cause a system to behave the way it does; only the material form of the representation is causally efficacious" [Pylyshyn 1984, p. 39].

I have, in this chapter, given some part of an account of how content may well have causal powers that do not supervene on those of some representation. But there are some philosophical loose ends yet to tie up; I'll return to those later, in chapter 10.

Arguments for internalism are always conceptual, metaphysical, or methodological. But the general strategy of trying to make questions into one where both answers make sense, and answering the question might tell you some real facts about the world—like in the units of selection case, as Sober casts it—might seem to leave the internalists in a weak position. It's not that no possible case could be mustered here; but as far as I can tell, none has been. Rather, they have tended toward either "what else could it be", or "look at all it's done". I am suggesting what else it could be; and the successes in research so far are neither so impressive as to be rested upon, nor (as I will argue soon) particularly reliant on some kind of internalist methodology.

But first, I'll take a slightly closer look at the general question of picking between levels of organization. Having raised the issue of making the selection of preferred levels of organization in explanation into a real and partially empirical one that might give different answers in different cases, as well as having opened up the possibility of critically context-dependent properties potentially being at the preferred level, I'll turn to the problem of filling out more how such questions might actually be raised and addressed in general.

CHAPTER
THREE

PICKING LEVELS

Having taken a preliminary look at the idea of the *autonomy* of higher-level organization and the linked notions of *multiple realizability* and *context-dependence*, let me turn now to the general question underlying the rejection of individualism in the previous chapter: How might we pick a "preferred" level of explanation for a given phenomenon? The importance of this question for current purposes is obvious: The central argument of this book is that the explanation of intelligence, thought, perception, and action will demand that we adopt explanatory frameworks that take thinker and world as a kind of interactive unit.

Questions about "preferred levels" recur across the sciences: in discussions of individualism and holism in the social sciences; genic, organismic, and group selection in evolutionary biology; and connectionist and cognitivist models in computational psychology. How are we to pick the appropriate level to explain a class of phenomena? What are we to make of apparent conflicts between explanations at different levels? Is there a way in which apparent conflicts might be transformed from verbal disputes into real, at least partially empirical questions—questions with solutions that avoid both the triviality of simplistic reductionism ("only the little individuals matter") and the vapidity of complete ecumenicalism ("any level—individualistic or holistic—is as good as another")? How is it that views advocating the importance of higher-level accounts avoid implying that (as Elliot Sober puts it) "you must add some sort of occult social fluid to individuals and their interactions to get social groups" [Sober 1984a, p. 185]?

In this chapter, I'll do three things: First, I'll take a brief pass at some background considerations involving the general idea of *higher-level causation*. Second, I'll consider a kind of strategy for picking between levels of explanation (based on one offered by Robert Brandon), and try to illustrate its plausibility and usefulness. And third, I'll suggest how this might help make sense of a notion of *distal* causation that I'll use later—especially in chapter 10.

3.1. Higher-Level Causation

A critical distinction to make about any higher-level property is whether the property is *epiphenomenal* or *causal* with respect to some specified class of effects. Some higher-level properties are trivially epiphenomenal with respect to some effects: The higher-level property of having a particular kind of information processing structure is epiphenomenal with respect to the causal power a particular computer has to break something when dropped. The mentioned higher-level properties make no direct causal contribution to the particular aspect of the system's behavior we've picked out; they are epiphenomenal with respect to those effects; the effects occur *in virtue of* other properties of the event.

Elliot Sober [1984b] gives a nice illustration of distinguishing causation *in virtue of* particular properties. There is a child's toy that consists of a sealed tube containing balls of various sizes, with each size of ball having a particular distinct color—green for the largest, black for the smallest, and so on. The tube is then sectioned off at regular intervals by gratings with various size openings—the coarsest grating nearest the top of the tube, the finest nearest to the bottom. Starting with all balls at the top of the tube, a little shaking will of course sort the balls into the various compartments by descending size, leaving the smallest (black) balls at the bottom.

As Sober points out, this sorting device provides selection *of* the black balls; but the selection is clearly not *for* the black balls, but *for* the *smaller* balls. The black balls reliably end up at the bottom of the tube, and thus the generalization that this will be so is straightforwardly true. But they end up there *in virtue of* being *small*; the causally potent property is their size, and not their color. The reliable generalization about color and eventual position is *spurious*; we might also characterize this by saying that the balls don't end up in those positions *in virtue of* their colors, or that their colors are *epiphenomenal* with respect to the causal processes leading to the positions. But the correlation between *size* and eventual position is *causal*—or if you prefer, eventual position is (at least partially) in virtue of size; size is *causally potent*. It's this latter sort of case that I'll call *higher-level property causation*.

It's sometimes suggested that the higher-level properties of systems are "real" and "in the world" only as "powers to produce effects on us as observers"—side-effects on perceivers of the potent lower-level causes, but not part of a real causal story about the system itself. I think this is a seriously misguided view of the position of higher-level properties in the world.

Consider some macro-level physical phenomena. Putnam [1973] asks the question: How can we explain why a 1" square peg won't go through a round hole 1" in diameter? Most naturally, it's explained in terms of the geometry of rigid objects. No good materialist denies that there is also an "explanation" (or at least a derivation from initial conditions and laws) of this particular event in terms of particle physics. But the macro-level explanation is a perfectly good one, and in fact has some familiar virtues over the microphysical one—primarily, the ability to generalize to an interesting natural class of cases. Further, there's a strong inclination to hold that it is *in virtue of* the rigidity of the peg and board that the one will not go through the other. Similarly for other macro-level physical phenomena: It is in virtue of the *temperature* inside the oven that it causes various chemical reactions to occur in the cake I'm baking; it is in virtue of the *acidity* of the solution that it takes the dirt off of the surface; and it is in virtue of the relatively *non-porous* nature of the cup that it holds the liquid.

Even to a fairly rabid reductionist, there's nothing particularly objectionable about saying that something happened in virtue of such innocuous higher-level properties because these are "really just physical properties" described in slightly more abstract terms.[1] To be rigid is just to have one of a large class of micro-physical structures; a class determined by . . . you know, how *rigid* the thing is. And to be at a temperature of $0°C$ is just to have molecules with a particular *mean* kinetic energy; the particular motions of the individual molecules being irrelevant. You might even think of taking the higher-level characterizations as giving "abbreviations" of a sort for the "real" micro-physical description—that is, characterizations of the phenomena that gloss away from many (for the moment

---

1. You *could* dig in your heels and insist that nothing *ever* happens *in virtue of* any properties other than those picked out by canonical descriptions in some ideal language of completed micro-physics. But this would require regarding as epiphenomenal properties that seem in some sense straightforwardly physical ones—having a given shape, chemical composition, temperature, and so on.

unimportant) details. Temperature *is* mean *MKE*, and to give the temperature is to characterize a certain complete micro-state of the object under consideration, albeit in a much more general and abstract way.

If the causal potency of these "innocuously higher-level properties" is allowed, and we accept that things sometimes really do have their effects in virtue of their temperature, rigidity and shape, chemical composition, and the like, we then need to answer the question of when higher-level property causation is "innocuous" and when it is not. For in spite of the failure of *general* higher-level epiphenomenalism, *sometimes* a higher-level analysis of a system postulates causally irrelevant properties of that system—as in the case of dropping the computer mentioned above. In general, what we'd like is an account of when a higher-level explanation is appropriate, and when it is not—that is, we'd like an answer to the general question of how to go about picking appropriate levels of organization for the explanation of various kinds of phenomena.

3.2. Brandon on Levels and Screening Off

Robert Brandon [1984] attempts to give an answer to this question of how to pick between levels of explanation—at least in the context of the units of selection controversy in the philosophy of biology. His account makes central use of the probabilistic notion of *screening off* in picking out the preferred level of organization for the explanation of particular effects. Although I find Brandon's account here clever and suggestive, I believe it ultimately fails. But I'll offer a revision that I believe avoids the problems of his account.

Screening off is a fairly intuitive idea: A screens off B from C iff the assumption of A makes B probabilistically irrelevant with respect to C, but not vice versa. In symbols, A screens off B from C iff $P(C/A\&B) = P(C/A) \neq P(C/B)$. Or to put it in a more intuitive but slightly less precise way: A screens off B from C just in case all the correlation between B and C is *in virtue of* their correlations with A.

It has been widely pointed out [see, for example, Salmon 1984] that the screening off relation captures some aspects of the direction and proximity of causation: First, common causes screen off common effects from one another; e.g., atmospheric pressure screens off barometer readings from inclement weather. Fix the pressure, and any variation in barometer reading will not further correlate with a varying likelihood of stormy weather. And second, more proximal causes in a chain screen off more distal ones from their common effects—e.g., gas pedal pressure and throttle position are both correlated with engine speed; but fix the causally intermediate variable of throttle position, and variations in gas pedal pressure no longer will correlate with changes in engine speed.

Brandon [1984] focuses on the fact that phenotypes screen off genotypes from the reproductive success of the individual organism: Fix the phenotypical properties of the organism, and variations in the genotype no longer correlate with reproductive success. He takes this to suggest more generally that screening off should be taken as marking which level of organization is *directly* responsible for particular effects. Entities or properties at the level of organization *directly* responsible for some particular effects should screen off entities or properties at other levels of organization from those effects. As he puts it for the case at hand: " . . . screening off provides us with the means for answering the question 'At what level does the causal machinery of organismic selection really act?' " [Brandon 1984, p. 135].[2]

But there is a clear limitation on Brandon's use of screening off in this context. Screening off might well capture the direction and proximity of causation in the original cases, but might still only be accidentally correlated with the question of preferred levels of organization in the genotype/phenotype case. This is because we can simply subsume the genotype/phenotype example under the general case of more proximal causes screening off more distal ones. Phenotypical properties are the more proximal causes of reproductive success; genotypical properties are relevant only as the more distal causes of those phenotypical properties. Phenotypes should screen off genotypes from reproductive success in virtue of being more proximal causes of those effects. The fact that they do should then by itself not be taken as offering any additional support for Brandon's view of *levels*. The data offered here are just what we'd expect simply from the fact that the phenotype is the more *proximal* cause.

---

2. No correlation alone will suffice to show causation, of course. But screening off here is not put forth as a complete criterion or definition of the causal relation we're after, but as a notable mark or indicator. Surely at least one other critical mark will be a kind of *projectibility* of the properties under consideration—a topic I'll return to in chapter 4.

The more common and interesting case of sorting levels is where *neither* level is more proximal to the effect in question than the other, but where they are in fact *token identical*; i.e., where the properties at the two levels in question are properties of the very same physical structure—unlike the case of genetic and phenotypical properties of organisms. What is there to say about cases where the relationship between the properties at different levels is one of token identity, and not of distinct points along a temporally ordered causal chain?

3.3. Multiple Realizability and Context-dependence

In the standard cases of causal proximity discussed earlier, it's clear how to think of holding one event or set of properties fixed while allowing another to vary: Since the two antecedent events or states are spatially and temporally distinct, we use this to isolate them. Fix the local and momentary properties of the event, and we can counterfactually vary the possible causal chains that might have led to that state of affairs. Fix the local properties of the bullet entering the body, and the effects of bodily damage are not further correlated with whether the bullet came from pulling the trigger or dropping the gun.

In the token identity case, we clearly need a substitute for spatio-temporal isolation along the causal chain. But with multiple realizability and context-dependence, we may have it. Multiple realizability allows local lower-level differences without higher-level differences: The same higher-level property can be instantiated by various lower-level configurations and materials. Conversely, context-dependence allows higher-level differences without local lower-level differences: The same local lower-level structure can instantiate various higher-level properties, depending on its context.

We can vary (counterfactually, that is—just as in the earlier cases) the lower-level implementation of the fixed higher-level properties by using the higher-level properties' multiple realizability. Fix some higher-level property of a structure—say, the throttle's properties as an air flow controller. Then whatever further lower-level properties that throttle may have (e.g., being a butterfly valve or a sideslip valve, being made of steel or aluminum, and so on) turn out to be independent of the effects of the throttle on engine speed. Those properties can then be seen as screening off lower-level implementational properties in much the same way as in the standard cases:

Fix the properties more *directly* responsible for the effect, and then note the independence of the effect from the various ways in which those properties might be produced—produced now not by different causal *histories*, but by different lower-level implementations.

So multiple realizability allows lower-level properties to be altered within the constraint of fixed higher-level properties. To conversely fix *lower*-level properties while allowing *higher*-level properties to vary we can use context-dependence.[3] Fix the *local* physical properties of a structure, and its higher level properties may still vary, depending on the surrounding context. So, if we specify the local physical structure of the choke in a carburetor, and then allow the surrounding context to vary, then whether it's still a choke or not will depend (among other things, of course) on its position vis-à-vis the fuel jets: If it's above the jets, it will control the richness of the fuel/air mixture, and will thus be a choke; but if it's *below* the jets in the new context, it will modulate the total amount of fuel/air mix going to the intake manifold, and will thus become a throttle. In fact, all the same sorts of examples given in chapter 2 are appropriate here: fix the chemical structure of a DNA molecule, and its *genetic* properties can still vary, depending on where in the overall genome it occurs, or on the particular nature of the coding mechanisms present; fix the machine-level properties of a given CPU operation in a computer, and its functional role in the higher-level program can still vary; and so on. So context-dependence allows for the possibility of lower-level properties of structures screening off their higher-level properties from some class of effects, and it does so in much the way that multiple realizability allowed in the possibility of higher-level properties of systems screening off the lower-level ones.

3.4. Examples and Applications

Let's try looking at a few examples to get clearer on how the current tools might be used. I'll look at three domains for higher-level explanations—evolutionary, computational, and linguistic. In each case, I'll try to bring out a fairly clear example where the lower-level account is preferable, and one where the higher-level account

---

3. Note that if the higher-level properties of components of complex systems were *not* context-dependent, fixing lower-level properties while varying the higher-level ones would be impossible—ruled out by supervenience.

is, and ask in each case how the offered tools might handle the situation.

Evolutionary. The discussion of the idea of *group selection* in the philosophy of biology has brought out some examples of clear cases where groups of organisms not only fit the fairly standard characterization of evolving [following Lewontin 1970], *heritable differential fitness*, but also fairly clearly fail to have their selective properties *in virtue of* being a group of that sort. So, for example, groups of animals that tend to run faster may have a selection advantage, but only because each individual organism is better off if it can run faster. Thus, the differential fitness of groups of animals that run fast is not a property for which groups are selected, but only one for which organisms are selected. Or to put it more in the current terms: A property of a group that correlates with the success of the group and its members may well be impotent, and simply an artifact of the truly efficacious properties—in this case, the strength of the individual organisms. This is just to say that some *group* fitness properties are epiphenomenal in the current sense—that is, they are not the properties in virtue of which the selection is taking place.

But not all higher-level selected properties are like this. Some properties are selected for only because of the advantage in survival and reproduction they confer on some entity; perhaps sometimes a group as a whole,[4] but even more clearly in the case of individual organisms. In fact, this is probably as clear an example as can be found of the causal potency of higher-level properties. The properties in virtue of which an organism survives and reproduces to whatever extent that it does are its *phenotypical* properties. What matters for its survival is, for example, how well its colors blend with its surroundings, and not what particular chemical combination it happened to use to achieve its coloration. The lower-level genetic causes are masked from the processes of selection by the phenotypical properties that they produce.

This is what Gould calls the "fatal flaw" with the view that all natural selection should be seen as a matter of selection for and survival and reproduction of particular *genes* rather than particular phenotypes: Genes are not directly visible to selection [Gould 1984]. Selection may favor strength, beauty, speed, aggressiveness, and the like. But there are not genes for these; these are instead

4. See Sober [1984a] for some nicely convincing cases.

complex emergent properties of genotypes. So individual genes aren't selected for, but complex alliances of genes may be. But genetic variants that have the same phenotypical results aren't distinguished between by selection. What matters for natural selection are—at least in large part—properties of organisms at the phenotypical level, regardless of the way in which they are genetically encoded. In such cases, the higher-level phenotypical properties then screen off the lower-level implementations: Fix the phenotypical properties; then which genetic variant they're implemented by will be irrelevant to the fitness of the organism.

Computational. As noted earlier, the multiple levels of organization in computational systems provide probably the most straightforward example we have of nested "virtual machines." It also is a particularly good domain in which to bring out the distinction between epiphenomenal and causally potent higher-level processes.

There are many good kinds of illustration here of processes that depend on lower-level phenomena but not higher-level ones—i.e., ones where the lower-level properties will mask those at the higher level from some particular set of effects. Let me just focus on one particular sort of case here—on a particular kind of disfunction. Consider a case where a particular higher-level event in a computer (e.g., its finding the value of list L) causes a system crash because of the lower-level properties of that particular event (e.g., it stores data at a particular real memory location which is physically disfunctioning). In this case, the event of finding that value would cause the crash; but not *in virtue of* that higher-level property—rather, it would cause that crash purely in virtue of its lower-level properties. Which higher-level event it was is *accidental* with respect to the consequences in this case; it doesn't matter which it was, only that it had the lower level property of using that particular real memory location. That is to say: The contextual properties of the lower-level event that make it also an instantiation of the higher-level event of finding the value of list L might be varied so as to alter the higher-level properties of the event, but that variation will be masked by the local lower-level properties from the effects in question.

In contrast, the normal case of causation in the computer is one where the higher-level properties do matter. So, for example, consider the case where the occurrence of a command PRINT ''Hello world'' in a BASIC program leads in the normal way to the words "Hello world" being displayed on the screen. That command caused that output in virtue of being that kind of BASIC instruction. There are many ways to implement such a command at the lower (machine-language) level; *any* of them would have been fine, and would have had the same results, as long as it had been an instance of ''PRINT 'Hello World' '' in that particular computational context. What matters is that it is a BASIC instruction of that sort. The class of lower-level states which could implement that instruction in that context is bounded, of course (e.g., it must be suited to the CPU used, the structuring of memory, etc.). But the implementational variants are irrelevant to (i.e., masked from) the effect of printing.

Linguistic. Consider the question of taxonomy necessary for dealing with language so that we might be able to accomplish anything like translation. It would be absurd to try to accomplish translation with a finer-grained characterization than that of something like the word, or at least the morpheme—e.g., on a letter-by-letter, phoneme-by-phoneme, or acoustical basis.[5] There are clearly interesting facts about language (e.g., that "dog" and "building" are both nouns, and that "it's pretty" means the same thing as "es bonita") that *cannot* be captured by those finer-grained analyses. And again, the intuitive fit with the "screening off" analysis is clear: Consequences in contexts of translation are determined by words (and even higher-level structures); variations in implementational orthographic properties are masked. But the consequences of the occurrence of a word where the operations done on it are done on letters (as in a spelling checker, or a simple text sorter) will be masked from variations in meaning by the orthographic properties of the word.

The observation that any attempt to translate on, say, a letter-by-letter basis is doomed to failure brings out an interesting point. The reason you can't do the translation is *not* (primarily) because of any context-relativity of the function of letters. (They have *some* context relativity in terms of their contribution to the sound of the word, but this isn't the real problem.) It would be absurd to suggest that we could actually translate letter by letter if only we would take the context relativity of letters into effect. "You just have to keep in mind that 'e' in 'pretty' has to be translated as 'o' in the

5. Of course, I think that facts about context are critical too, actually. But the weaker claim will be plenty for now.

'pretty/bonita' context." The roles of letters are to contribute to a certain orthographic structure; but only some small class of these orthographic structures are the sorts of things that are meaningful at all, and thus become candidates for translation. Unless the chunks are of the right sort, the question of translation cannot even be raised, and thus it's absurd to see letters as making any independent contribution to the meanings of terms—even a kind of context-dependent contribution (as when the contribution of an air flow valve as choke or as throttle is a context-dependent fact about it [see Quine 1953]).

Why then *is* letter-by-letter translation absurd? Because the context here is *everything*. We would no doubt in principle be able to characterize translation between words as translation between letters with context-dependent properties. But the contexts would turn out to be, essentially, "occurs in the word——" for each word containing that letter that we could translate. Clearly this is just a notational variant of a scheme that translates word by word, and one that only inserts superfluous complexity.

3.5. Causation at a Distance?

I've suggested how to make sense of screening off as a key to preferred levels even when the property at the preferred level isn't more proximal to the effect than the competitor. By making use of multiple realizability and context-dependence, we can use the tool to help sort out the issues even when the properties at the various levels are token identical. But I'd like to turn to making a slightly stronger claim. Not only can the idea of screening off be used without taking advantage of causal proximity; it can be used even when the property at the "preferred" level of organization is *more distal* than those at other levels of organization.

On the face of it, this should seem odd for two obvious reasons: One is that screening off was originally used here as a marker of explicit causal proximity: More proximal causes mask more distal ones. The other is that the priority of distal (over proximal) causation might naturally be thought of as the heart of the idea of *occult* causation. But what I'd like to try to do in this section is to show how we might make sense of the *prima facie* counterintuitive possibility of *distal* causes sometimes screening off more proximal ones. One reason for this is just to finish up the account of screening off and causal levels; but another is to set up the discussion of *intentional* and *teleological* causation in chapter 10.

We saw above how properties at one level of organization could mask token identical properties by taking advantage of multiple realizability and context-dependence to fix some properties while allowing those at another level to vary. How might we similarly try to make sense of the idea of a more distal cause screening off a more proximal one from the effect? As a first try: The distal cause screens off the more proximal one just in case fixing the distal cause fixes the effect across variation in proximal cause—that is, across variations in the route by which the distal cause has its effect on the system.

Of course, this won't be *regardless* of the proximal route. In the cases where we used multiple realizability to fix the higher-level properties while varying those at the lower level, we had to constrain the variation. The idea there was that the lower-level properties could be varied within the bounds of the fixed higher-level properties. A similar constraint here might be that the variations should be compatible with distal causation of the effect. So I'm suggesting that the distal cause is preferred over the more proximal one if the effect correlates with the distal cause regardless (more or less) of the precise route by which that distal cause has its proximal effects.

An example will help. An organism might be selected for its camouflage; blending into the background helps it avoid predators. But there are lots of routes by which the match and mismatch with the environment has its effects on the organism's reproductive success—different predators, different particular locations, etc. If there were only one route by which the match with the environment had its effect, then explaining the effect in terms of more proximal causation along that route might be preferable. But in the case of multiple lower-level causal routes to the same effect, where the match with the environment has its effects regardless of which of the various possible routes of causation is in effect, there won't be a lower-level more proximal cause that will capture the same generality—the same class of effects. Fix the match/mismatch, and the effect follows regardless of the details of the causal route; the class of variations across which the effect is fixed is a natural class of *distal* states and *not* of *proximal* ones.[6]

The heart of the idea is that distal causes can screen off proximal ones by exhibiting the more appropriate level or grain of taxonomy than the proximal ones for the account of the systematicities to be explained. As with the cases of token identity, there's an important sense in which what we're doing is specifying *type* causation—that is, we're saying *in virtue of which properties* a particular event or object causes some specified effects. And there may well be cases in which there are no more proximal properties in virtue of which a particular *class* of effects takes place, even if each *case* in that class has some more proximal cause at a lower level of organization.

I think that it's no accident that it is cases of *intentional* and *teleological* causation where we will most typically see the importance of distal higher-level causes. These are, after all, cases where causation is specified in terms of *objects* or *goals* of the process that are spatially and/or temporally distal. But that's an issue I'll put off until chapters 9 and 10, where I'll deal with perception and intentional causation.

I began by noting that the problem of picking the most appropriate level or levels of explanation of the behavior of complex systems spans many explanatory domains, including the social sciences, biology, and the computational sciences of the mind. The goal was to find a general strategy for the analysis and possible resolution of apparent conflicts between various explanatory levels without taking false solace in either simplistic reductionism or complete ecumenicalism. I suggested further that in allowing at least the *possibility* that the "preferred" level in particular cases be some higher level of organization, any such strategy should also suggest how this kind of higher-level dominance avoids the implication of any kind of non-mechanical or occult view of causation.

But with any meta-theoretical explanatory framework, the real proof of the pudding should be in the eating. Will it help make sense of the real issues we face in this domain? I've suggested how

6. If you're tempted to turn toward a bizarre counterfactual characterization of the proximal stimulus, see Sober and Lewontin [1984] for a discussion (in the context genic-level accounts of natural selection) of why such conversions from properties of higher-level entities to grossly "context-dependent" properties of their components both introduce unneeded complexity for no gain, and mischaracterize the *causes* of the process at work by replacing them with lower-level *artifacts* of notation.

it makes sense of some of the cases that seem moderately straight-forward at this point in time. What I'll turn to in the next section of the book is bringing it to bear—along with some of the other morals of the past three chapters—on the particular instance of a problem in choosing between theoretical stances which is the real focus of this project: that of the relative merits of "internalist" and "embedded" conceptions of thought and intelligence.

PART TWO

Bounding and Embedding

CHAPTER
FOUR

THE FRAME
PROBLEMS

At this point, I will move the discussion to the domain of information-processing explanation of complex behavior, and consider why we should be unhappy with the internalist status quo. I will try to synthesize a set of concerns about the possibility of Artificial Intelligence in particular into a unified problem for non-embedded accounts. I'll characterize the generalized *frame* problem as containing the two distinct problems of the *under-determination* of hypothesis by data, and the *overconstraint* on inference faced in dealing with a complex and dynamic task. I'll also examine how human agents seem to deal with the resulting problems of bounding of search and inference strategies with heuristics that trade fairly robust and systematic failure patterns in some contexts for some pretty dramatic "bounding" of the process of deliberation. And I'll begin to look at how the reasonableness of a strategy for bounding inference is, like the projectibility of predicates in a taxonomy, relative to the world that the strategy or taxonomy is applied to.

In the next chapter, I'll explicate further the notion of *bounded* rationality (or, sometimes, *satisficing*), and suggest an extension and reconceptualization of its typical application in this context. Even given the widespread explicit appeals to "bounded" rationality in AI, the rhetoric of *optimality* often lurks only slightly beneath the surface. Boundedness is often misconstrued as a kind of variant on optimization which calculates in further information involving projections about the effects of limitation of the machine (e.g., hardware constraints, information availability, possible lost opportunities for action, and so on)—that is, as *optimizing under constraints*. Such a use of "boundedness" strategies directs us away from the kind of application of boundedness which may provide a schema for dealing with some central problems in AI—in particular, the generalized frame problem. It gives the wrong idealization to take as a *task* account of the kind of rational inference that problem-solvers must engage in.

And in chapter 6, I'll turn to considering how we might begin to place greater dependence on implicitly exploiting the contingent regularities in the environment in strategies for dealing with a complex and dynamic world. By exploiting the interactivity between organism and environment, we might discover ways to tailor the actions of the organism more appropriately and effectively to the contingencies of the particular kind of environment it faces—a task I'll then fill out in more detail throughout part III of this book.

4.1. Two Problems in One

There is some degree of ambiguity and confusion as to what is really meant by the "frame" problem in AI. In the present discussion, what I am concerned with is the frame problem broadly construed—taken not as a local and technical problem, but as a very general meta-theoretical or epistemological problem. As Daniel Dennett [1984] puts it, it is a new epistemological problem that work in AI has brought us face to face with.

There are really two very distinct issues of concern within the common notion of the generalized frame problem. The two notions correspond roughly to the problem of inference and projection as *underdetermined* and as *overconstrained*. More specifically, the first problem is the general theoretical problem of inductive inference: How do you pick a conclusion or general principle when the data available doesn't determine anything like a unique choice? This is the puzzle of *projectibility* in the philosophy of science, or if you prefer, the problem of the *underdetermination of theory by data*. And the second problem is that of dealing with situations where there are clearly more tasks than resources, and where devoting informational resources to one job means not devoting them to another potentially rewarding task. The first is in some sense clearly more of a theoretical question about the nature of inductive inference; while the latter is closer to a kind of pragmatic question of engineering machines to deal with particular real-world constraints.

I'm not suggesting that these questions are unrelated. One of the reasons that there is so much to do (and thus the domain is overconstrained) is that *inductive inference* seems so hard without anything like a general account of how it is that we might find a way to constrain inference. Further, the two questions might seem like, respectively, a question about *competence* and one about *performance*. This idea—that at least some part of the frame problem arises not just in the performance account of the system, but in the content or substance theory as well—is critical, and will receive significant attention in the next chapter. But first, let me focus in turn on the two aspects of the frame problem I've separated here: first, on the general problem of underdetermination in inductive inference; and second, on the way in which the problem of generating intelligent action is overconstrained and thus pushes us toward more bounded conceptions of rationality.

4.2. Underdetermination, Taxonomy, and Induction

Our first problem at hand is the very general one of the underdetermination of hypothesis by data: There is no principled way to pick between the multiplicity of hypotheses which will be compatible with any finite body of data. Which regularities project into future cases? Which curve should we draw through a finite set of points? Which correlations are non-spurious? The problem has been put in many ways: from Hume's worries about what additional principle is needed to go from a pattern of observations to a projection about future cases, to discussions about the justification of the assumption of the "regularity of nature" in this century, to Goodman's "new riddle of induction" about differentiating projectible and non-projectible predicates [Goodman 1954]. According to the current epistemological conventional wisdom, the underlying problem in all of these discussions is one that has no principled and general solution.[1]

To put the problem in what seems for many people to be its most intuitive form: You have some data points on the graph. What curve do you draw? Any finite set of points can be mapped by an infinite number of possible curves. Adding points still leaves an infinite number, ad infinitum. The data won't pick the curve if the possibilities are unconstrained by anything else. Of the infinite number of ways to taxonomize a situation (or if you like, curves to draw through the data points), which should be picked for projection? Once we've exhausted the influence of the data, what else is there?

---

1. The classic piece on this puzzle is of course Goodman's "The New Riddle of Induction" [Goodman 1954]. But perhaps the best recent discussion of the general issue here can be found in Sober [1988], especially chapter 2.

That there's no "in-principle" way to do this obviously doesn't mean it never gets done. We in fact do pick curves and accomplish inductive inference all the time. How do we manage this to the extent that we do? One very natural suggestion about how this problem gets solved is roughly via some notion of *simplicity*. We pick the simplest curve that goes through the point; we accept the least complex correlation, and make the inference which is the least convoluted. But this is not giving an answer. Simplicity is clearly a function of the taxonomy and coordinate system being used, and our task is to find a way to pick *these*.

There probably is no more resounding moral in the philosophy of science in the last 40 years than this: Hypothesis precedes data. The vaguely Baconian idea that data collection proceeds in some way prior to the formation of the hypothesis to be checked—and especially, prior to the taxonomy which that hypothesis imposes—has been trounced repeatedly in the second half of this century. And even when some notion of observation prior to theory formulation is advocated [see, for example, Hacking 1983], it's seen as a kind of exception to a pattern—an example of an over-extension of the general story rather than an overturning of it. Without some way to taxonomize the data so that the intractable chaos of the world can be pared down to some manageable body of data, we don't know what to look at, record, track, and base our inferences on.

This issue also arises not just from the perspective of what we should do ourselves in performing inductive inferences, but also in how we see the process of inductive learning when examining the behavior of organisms. To use an example of Dennett's: Why does slapping the child's hand when she reaches into the cookie jar tend to keep her out of the cookie jar (at least when you're around) rather than discouraging her from performing any of the multitude of other behaviors she was performing at that moment—e.g., standing on one foot, raising her arm, etc.? Or for that matter, any of the other things she's done recently that you might be punishing her for? So one central aspect of the "underdetermination" aspect of the frame problem is the general problem of finding projectible predicates— of finding the right vocabulary with which to carve the world. But which correlation you should project is dependent on what *else* you know about the system.

And not just globally, in that you need to know *something* other than bare correlations to determine which correlations are projectible. It's even worse than that. The most difficult problem for producing a "preferred taxonomy" is that projectibility is context-dependent. How you project beyond the data can be highly contingent on the structure of the situation. Exactly the same strength of correlation so far will allow for projection in one case but not another. For projections about digit span in short-term memory, the height of the subject is assumed (reasonably) to be irrelevant. But the assumption that height is not relevant to generalizations about sports preference would be clearly tendentious. And the most critical aspect of our knowledge in a context which informs and guides inductive inference is our knowledge of the underlying *mechanism* at work.

For example, take the generalization that typed papers tend to get better grades. Suppose we have noted a perfectly good correlation that, say, the mean grade for typed papers is one letter grade higher than for handwritten papers. Whether this generalization is projectible in the obvious context of interest ("should I type my paper to raise my chances of getting a good grade?") is of course entirely contingent on what I think the *mechanism* for the correlation is. If it's that the person grading the papers is harsher on handwritten papers (for whatever reason—resents their being harder to read, assumes the student didn't work very hard, whatever), then the correlation *should* be projected—typing your paper *will* raise your chances of a good grade. But if the mechanism is one of preselection for who normally types papers (non-typed papers are on average going to come from students who worked less hard, were rushed, didn't care, etc.) then the correlation *shouldn't* be used. In that case, the mechanism of the correlation only works in selecting which papers on average get typed, and not on what happens to a given paper—typed or not—once it's handed in.

So mechanism is absolutely critical. The only possible way that you can do induction is by having the right kind of background of knowledge that provides you some sense of the mechanisms of the correlation—or if you prefer, allows you in some way to find which things should be taken as independent for present purposes. The way that we actually accomplish induction is by knowing (without considering) which independence assumptions should be made. It's not the combinatorials that make real inductions work and at the same time tend to be hard to figure out. The study of complex combinatorials is the study of problems and solutions against the background of a fixed taxonomy, and that's exactly what we *don't* have. In this way, the puzzle really is the underdetermination of taxonomy problem that has been made salient in the philosophy of science over the last 40 years.

4.3. Overconstraint and the Art of Ignoring

But it isn't enough to have a global solution to the problem of inductive inference—to know how to decide how to pick the right hypothesis given a set of data. You might be able to decide on the relationship between any piece of data and a hypothesis but not be able to solve the frame problem. You not only need to be able to decide the relationship in whatever cases you might consider; you also need to know which things to consider. You can't check them all; the problem has to be made tractable. Even if there is some algorithm for going from one complete characterization of a set of data and rules to a new such set on the basis of new information, we would still face the problem of doing it under real constraints of speed, competition for resources, and a changing world.

This aspect of the frame problem is one about *constraining* computation *relative to real-world complexities and real-time constraints*, and so the question can't *just* be one of how we determine relevance when we explicitly consider a particular bit of information. If we have to consider explicitly everything in the database (and iterations of connections), then we haven't constrained computation, and thus haven't solved the problem—even if we have developed an effective procedure for explicit evaluation of each item. So even *with* an answer to the generalized problem of idealized inductive inference, the problem of real and limited inference machines remains. What we need is a way to establish search and inference procedures that implicitly determine relevance *without looking*. If you have to look at everything, you haven't saved time and effort. We need to find a way to establish intelligent procedures that reliably *ignore* what's irrelevant *without explicitly considering it*.

Taken in the broadest sense, the general form of the problem is just this: How do we decide/know when to stop thinking and start acting? How do we decide when we've looked enough before we leap? How do we find the appropriate amount of thought, planning, computation, and information search to engage in so we can do the right thing, but still do it in real time? Or as Jerry Fodor [1987b] has put it: How do we solve (and get machines to solve) Hamlet's problem? This part of the problem is one of knowing which paths to ignore, and thus constraining search; of knowing when to stop thinking and to go ahead and act.

Note that shifting the problem to the acquisition side doesn't help here. If you set things up so that when the time for actual inference comes up, only some small set of possible changes in fact gets considered (as in McDermott's [1987] "sleeping dog" strategy), you simply have the same problem in setting up what gets used and what gets ignored at the time of setting the taxonomy, or at the time of knowledge acquisition when the links to other facts are established. It's not that, say, a strategy of inference that relies heavily on constrained search and backwards chaining to update the database might not be a part of the eventual engineering of the inference machine. It's just that the logical problem of determining what's to be ignored isn't avoided by such strategies.

4.4. Strategies and Errors

As I noted earlier, the kind of solution to the general problem of inductive inference which seems at least vaguely promising is the one which Sober calls giving an "ontological" account, which in AI is more commonly referred to as giving a "content theory." The solution, on this approach, is not to be found in cleverly jockeying around some account of the syntax of inductive inference. Rather than giving the magical general premise that is missing for inductive argument in general, we try to give some account of the particular structure of the world which, in the case of the inductive inference in hand, justifies the projectibility of the generalization—typically, by postulating at least some kind of schema for a mechanism by which the generalization holds.

And as for the problem of overconstraint: In its most general form, the point where search and inference should stop and ignoring should begin must be something like this: Don't use resources dealing with information which is either (a) actually independent of any of the projections that we're making, or (b) such that the cost of gathering any of this relevant information is high enough that it actually isn't worth getting. The question is one of whether the real time and real processing constraints of the task are such that it's not going to be productive to search out and calculate in further information. But to say this isn't to solve anything, but merely to restate the problem.

It's not, of course, that we never fail at this task, or that we never go down the wrong path or get the answer wrong in some way or other. But we manage in a lot of cases to get by; and sacrificing some accuracy for some extra tractability will often be a reasonable strategy. After all, a representation of the world in terms of its fundamental physics will be accurate, but entirely unusable in any real case. Not only is it intractable in terms of the complexity of calculation, but it's also ruled out by the conditions of informational constraint vis-à-vis the world under which we live. We simply don't have access to that kind of information about our environment by interacting with it. You often don't even know what's over the next hill.

So the problem is one of getting a strategy for ignoring and reasoning that is both accurate enough and manageable. How good, though? How effective a strategy for ignoring irrelevant data without overlooking what's significant should we expect? As a start toward getting a grip on that, let me review a couple of facts about human propensities to ignore even highly relevant data.

There's a robust tendency in human inference to apply a *representativeness* heuristic when making assessments of probabilities or likelihoods. When faced with a problem of the general form "how likely is it that *a* is an *F*?", we seem typically to make this judgement by assessing how *representative* or *typical a* is of *F*'s. This strategy is clearly of a piece with some of the well-known results on categorization and prototypicality [see Rosch and Mervis 1975]. Furthermore, noticing the use of this strategy gives a good account of an extremely general bias toward a particular systematic error in the assessment of conjunctive probabilities.

If probability assessments are made by simply assessing representativeness, this will clearly create a systematic pattern of failure in the assessment of *conjunctive* probabilities—that is, in assessing the likelihood of meeting both of two distinct conditions, even given a reasonable assessment of the likelihood of meeting each of the conditions independently. After all, meeting the conjunction of two conditions will always be no more likely than meeting the least likely of the two conditions: It's a logical precondition on satisfying the conjunction that you must satisfy the least likely conjunct, and adding the other requirement can only narrow down the possibilities further. But adding more conditions can *increase* the degree to which a particular item is *representative* of a class.

Widespread mistakes in reasoning involving the use of a representativeness heuristic and the resultant over-assessment of conjunctive probabilities are now a well-established psychological result. The work of Tversky and Kahneman and their colleagues is the best-known, and the effects shown are robust and consistent across a variety of cases:

The Conjunction Fallacy. Tversky and Kahneman [1982] characterize the "conjunction fallacy" of assessing the likelihood of conjunctions as being *higher* than that of the least likely conjunct. After being given some facts about a character named "Linda" which have been designed to imply that she might be a feminist, subjects robustly assess the likelihood of "Linda is a feminist bank teller" as higher than that of "Linda is a bank teller"—a clear violation of the conjunction principle in probability—even when they can perfectly well see that the conjunction rule in the abstract is correct.

Disregarding Base Rates. Tversky and Kahneman [1974] also illustrate the robust tendency to disregard base rates in probabilistic inference. In the best-known example, subjects were presented with the following problem: Jones lives in a city where 85% of the cabs are green and 15% are blue. He sees a cab in a hit-and-run accident one night, and says it looked like a blue one. We test him under similar perceptual conditions, and find that he correctly recognizes blue cabs 80% of the time (and takes them to be green the other 20% of the time), and similarly for green cabs: right 80%, wrong 20%. When asked for a guess about the color of the cab, most subjects incorrectly guess blue. This is the natural guess if a representativeness heuristic is used: The data—the witness saying the cab was blue—is typical of the cases where the cab was in fact blue, and atypical of the cases where it was in fact green. But if the "a priori" probability that the cab was green is fixed by the base rate (and is thus .85), and if 20% of the cabs would be misidentified with respect to their color, then the probability is $.85 \times .2 = .17$ that he saw a green cab but took it to be blue, while the probability that he saw a blue cab and took it to be blue is $.15 \times .8 = .12$. So it's more likely that he saw a green cab and misidentified it than that he saw a blue cab and correctly identified it. The subjects seem again to ignore the relevant information about the base rate in favor of using a shortsighted representativeness heuristic.

Misperception of Random Sequences. The use of a representativeness heuristic also contributes toward a bias to misperceive random sequences. Gilovich et al. [1985] show that the widespread and robust bias toward a belief in "streak" shooting in basketball is without statistical foundation, but that it is also a natural consequence of the general tendency toward the use of representativeness in probability judgements. Using representativeness as the measure of likelihood, it's natural to judge the series (letting H and M stand for "hit" and "miss," respectively) $MMHHHHHMMM$ as a less likely random sequence from a 50% shooter than the sequence $HMMHMHHMHM$ (the latter being a fairly typical-seeming random sequence, the former being atypical). Being seen as less likely, they further take this to suggest that it's less likely to be a random 50% sequence and more likely to have some underlying cause.

Representativeness isn't the only well-established heuristic which inserts significant biases in probabilistic reasoning. Another is that of *availability*. By assessing the probability of an event by depending on how available or easily recalled instances of such a type of event could be brought to mind, we'll overassess the likelihood of strikingly memorable types of events. *Anchoring* also provides significant bias where people make estimates by starting from some initial assessment and then adjusting toward the final answer the initial assessment will have a dominant effect on the eventual evaluation. Anchoring can, hand-in-hand with representativeness, account for the tendency to overestimate the probability of conjunctive accounts. By insufficiently adjusting from the initial probability of the primitive conjuncts, we don't drop the probability of the conjunction significantly enough.

In any case, the fact seems to be that in real belief fixation, we not only typically fail to bring to bear evidence from distant domains which may be in principle relevant, we also often fail to bring to bear evidence that is quite closely related to the problem, and which we have had explicitly pointed out to us. I'm not saying that this is *stupid*, or anything of the sort. In fact, as I'll suggest in the next chapter, it might be wise to design a system to work this way as an overall strategy. The current point is just that this heuristic—like all heuristics[2]—has systematic failure characteristics, and this one

---

2. See the discussion in Wimsatt [1986] for a clear look at some of the general properties of heuristics.

fails by systematically ignoring relevant and seemingly available information in cases like the ones above.

These kinds of phenomena might then suggest that the ways in which we deal with the bounding of search and inference is to use strategies and heuristics that trade some clear and systematic failure patterns in some contexts for some pretty dramatic boundedness. Ignoring the kind of information which is easily used, relevant, and in the case at hand, even cued by name in studies that ask for *probability* judgements, is a pretty noticeable bit of ignoring. But it's also one that, as a more general rule of thumb, may turn out to be an extremely reasonable heuristic to apply across the board as a strategy for ignoring, and thus dealing with a part of the frame problem. If the typical case where we face the task of making some kind of probability assessments is one where we *don't* have an explicitly conjunctive probability, or where we don't have ready knowledge of base rates, or where the search for the further relevant information is going to take, on average, more resources than it's worth, then the strategy will be a reasonable one.

The moral of the story is that the reasonableness of a strategy for inference is, like the projectibility of predicates in a taxonomy, relative to the world the strategy or taxonomy is applied to. But if this is so, what should we make of the idea of globally *solving* the problems of underdetermination and overconstraint in inference? How do we manage, and what idealizations about our strategies and abilities should be made to explain and perhaps duplicate our skills? It's to that question and its relationship to the more general idea of *bounded rationality* that I'll now turn.

BOUNDEDNESS
AND
CONTINGENCY

The notion of *satisficing* and the more general idea of *bounded rationality* have been around since Simon's landmark book, *Administrative Behavior* [Simon 1957]. Noting both the in-principle impossibility of ideal and optimal rationality, as well as the extent to which humans themselves fall short of it, Simon offers an alternative view of rationality that is to be taken as both descriptive and normative.

Although the general account is sometimes referred to as "satisficing," this is not quite accurate. The notion of "bounded rationality" is the most general one. Strategies for bounded rationality are *heuristics*—i.e., non-guaranteed strategies or "rules of thumb" for guiding problem-solving. "Satisficing," although sometimes used as a stand-in for the more general conception of boundedness, is really a particular subclass of heuristics or strategies for bounded rationality. To "satisfice" is to set some particular standard of outcome as "good enough" and to constrain the costs of inference and information search by stopping once you get an outcome at least that good. Although this is surely one way to structure a strategy for boundedness, it's hardly the only one: setting limits on time, making inferences from the usefulness of the search so far, setting limits on propagation of information through a network, or some hybrid of these and/or others—all are possible bounded strategies.

5.1. Facing Your Limitations

Bounded rationality is intended to cope with two central sources of constraint in virtue of which (as Simon puts it) "exact solutions to the optimization problems of the real world are simply not within reach or sight" [Simon 1981a, p. 36]. First, the limits on the calculation capabilities available for solving the problem: The process of reasoning must be accommodated to the limitations on the reasoner with respect to the tasks faced. The limitations on the thinker—e.g., the speed with which it can reason, or the limitations on memory size and/or accessibility—are facts that play a central role in determining which strategies are better than others for solving problems (e.g., if you're a plodder but never forget anything, don't use a strategy that emphasizes lots of inference over, say, storing lots of partially redundant information).

Second, the structure of the environment and uncertainties about it are also critical for determining rational strategies. Under uncertainty, questions arise about the depth of search, the time to seek new information, the rapidity with which opportunity is lost, and so on—all factors in the *environment*. So, for example, suppose the environment is such that there are many opportunities for moderate gain which are somewhat fleeting, but such that if grasped, take low risk and low investment of time and effort (e.g., reaching out and grabbing the fly as it buzzes by). Then the decision procedure which determines that an action is called for on the basis of very shallow reasoning will be a highly productive one—particularly if by acting the tendency is neither to take on further risks and costs nor forgo many other opportunities for more profitable action. As when I search for a car to buy, the decision of whether the best one so far is good enough or whether I should instead continue to search depends primarily on the nature of the environment that I will face as I search further. But it's exactly the information I would get from that further search and perhaps don't yet have that would let me make a well-informed judgement about whether further search is the right strategy in the context. This "catch 22" is common in trying to accommodate rational strategy to a relatively unknown environment. An informed meta-level decision about search strategy requires just the kind of information typically acquired via further search.

It's critical here to be careful about the differences between procedures used *by* a system in the course of its operation and those used *in the design* of such a system. Particular strategies for bounded rationality may well be in use at the point of design but not at the point of execution. A system may be built to work *in accordance with* some general principle or strategy (say, avoiding additional inferences in favor of searching the environment for more information) because the designer knows that a system with the particular capabilities available in this case (e.g., better at perception than at more abstract inference) will, in general, be better off favoring its strengths (at least in a suitably accommodating environment). But the system needn't at any point explicitly represent or use that rule. The procedures for weighing options might just be set up so as to accord with the appropriate task account that specifies the general logic of the strategy. The strategy would then be explicit in the design principles of the system, but only implicit in its implementation.

This might be a natural way to see biases in reasoning like those involving the use of a representativeness heuristic discussed at the end of the last chapter. The strategy of judging likelihoods by representativeness needn't be one which we explicitly represent. We might just be built (and perhaps trained) so that we just do it. Such a strategy should, in that case, be made explicit in the design and analysis of the system, but needn't be a principle used by the system in execution. Such an implicit strategy might also be an entirely reasonable design decision. Rather than searching for base rate information or deciding whether to use representativeness in each case, just construct the system so that it does it well and automatically, thus reducing the complexity of the decision at execution time. Under a wide class of circumstances (e.g., where explicit base rates are hard to get, where causal knowledge is impoverished, etc.), the strategy will work pretty well; and it's not implausible that the savings in resources—given considerations of overconstraint—will more than pay for the occasional errors to which the heuristic is vulnerable.

In AI, bounded rationality has played a critical role, even when not made explicit. Research has largely centered around the search for heuristics or strategies for bounded rationality which accomplish complex tasks without having to run algorithms which take practically forever (e.g., a brute force algorithm for chess). The problems of overconstraint and underdetermination arise through the surprising complexity of even "simple" tasks; and the real-time and information-gathering restrictions on machines have made this orientation plausible, obvious, and now essentially ubiquitous.

Central uses to which the strategy of bounded rationality are put in AI include those of considering hardware limitations on speed and memory, external constraints on the availability and cost of information, or even real-time constraints on the need to plan and decide quickly enough to take advantage of relatively fleeting opportunities for action in a changing environment. These are clearly important constraints that some kind of boundedness strategy must be used to deal with. In fact, some of the problems here may be more critical and pervasive than is typically imagined—particularly, in my view, that of constraints on availability of important information for decision-making.

5.2. Satisficing as Optimizing

Boundedness, when taken in all the ways listed above, might still be seen as a kind of *variant on optimization:* we optimize, but figure into the calculation various projections about hardware constraints, information availability, possible lost opportunities for action, and so on. Thus, the optimal course of action (i.e., the one with the highest expected utility) is determined by calculations using information which includes not only facts about the probabilities and utilities of various states in the environment, but also facts about how fast the machine can consider possibilities; an estimate of the changes in utility for the action which might be produced by delays in deciding (e.g., if you delay, somebody else might usurp your opportunity to act); the likelihood that not focusing on other actions during that period might cost you in lost opportunities; the expected values of those opportunities; and so on. In short, we figure the optimal course of action given the real constraints on the machine, and constrain our search for more relevant information (whether in memory or in the environment) and our further extrapolating of conclusions from the data in hand in the light of these factors.

Work like that of Stuart Russell [1989; Russell and Wefald 1989] on the use of a Bayesian decision-theoretic framework for knowledge and inference representation is representative of this notion of boundedness. The use of the notions of boundedness is still in the end combined with a fundamental adherence to a kind of idealization to some notion of optimality, and of picking the *best* possible option. [See Russell 1989, p. 17.] As Russell puts it himself, "we see the AI problem as that of designing systems capable of achieving optimal behavior (in a decision-theoretic sense) under computational constraints in complex task environments . . . " [Russell and Wefald 1989, p. 334]. And to accomplish this, "computations are . . . selected according to expected utility just as with ordinary action in the world," thus allowing us to "apply decision theory to provide a principled basis for metareasoning" [Russell 1989, p. 19]. As a result, the claim is made that "we have explicitly captured the real-time nature of the environment by explicitly including the situation in which an action is taken in the argument to the utility function. Such a comprehensive function of the total state of affairs captures all constraints and trade-offs . . . " [Russell 1989, p. 335]. On this view, boundedness is still then clearly seen as a kind of variant on optimization—we optimize, but take as part of the calculation projections about hardware constraints, information availability, possible lost opportunities for action, and so on.[1] As Steve Hanks [1990] nicely puts the idea, "spend a unit of time in deliberation if the expected marginal benefit of thinking exceeds the expected marginal cast of failing to act."

The problem is that on this approach, the problem-solver, at least on first pass, seems to end up taking even *more* information into account when deciding on actions—above and beyond that concerning the subject matter of the decision, the appropriate information concerning the speed of the agent's computations, the likelihood of finding relevant information by extending the search, the other tasks at hand and their relative importance, and so on. And this would seem, at least on the surface, to run exactly counter to the needs that the general frame problem places upon us—that of placing strong constraints on what's weighed. To put it one way: "Computing the opportunity cost associated with failure to act involves sophisticated reasoning about the hypothetical unfolding of events and about the agent's capabilities" [Hanks 1990, p. 6].

It's not that there couldn't in principle be domains in which such meta-reasoning at the point of execution might not save resources. It's that the real cases don't seem to be in that ballpark. In working out their own application of this strategy, Russell and Wefald [1989] acknowledge needing simplifying assumptions which entail "serious theoretical concerns": the *single-step assumption*, which constrains the meta-reasoning to only deal with the problem of whether *one* more search step is worthwhile; the use of *meta-greedy* algorithms, which assumes that the only value of a step is the one that shows up when it's completed, rather than including the facilitation of future action; and the assumption that the value of a step is the value of some single top-level goal, thus avoiding assessing conflicts and balance between goals. Clearly all three of these are assumptions that have exactly the consequence of avoiding the very concerns that the generalized frame problem has left us with.

---

1. As Russell put it very explicitly in a public lecture at the University of Chicago Artificial Intelligence Laboratory in late 1989: It's optimizing, modulo hardware constraints.

5.3. Boundedness without Optimization

The problem is that the critical failure in optimization has been missed. It is not directly an issue of hardware, as Russell suggested, or even of algorithm. It is instead one arising in something like what I called in chapter 1 the *task* account of the system, and the application of boundedness should go far beyond the sort suggested so far. The use of a notion of boundedness in the theory of the idealized task structure rather than just in the account of the realized procedural process is in fact a critical part of using boundedness and possibly providing at least a schema for dealing with the generalized frame problem.

A central point in chapter 1 was the importance of knowing *what* a complex system is doing in order to find out *how* it accomplishes that task—that is, we often need to know the function of complex system being analyzed to know what aspects of structure to look at. Determining overall significance and the sorting of noise from significant signal will depend on having some sense of the functioning of the system—of what the *task* account is supposed to give.

But task accounts also have their special pitfalls; a particularly significant one here is that of *overidealization*. Finding the appropriate idealization for systematicities in behavior of a complex system is *hard*. We often find ourselves searching for stability between the dangers of overidealization (resulting from giving up too much of the contingencies of behavior for some gain in elegance) and those of underidealization (resulting from striving for completeness at the cost of projectible systematicity). Overidealizations aren't unusual mistakes to make here; we've been lucky sometimes (as with ideal gases, where real gases sufficiently approximate collections of point masses for the laws to be a good approximation), but unlucky others (as with economics, where real "optimizing market agents" don't even read the labels).

As Simon [1981a, p. 37] says, "the behavior of an [adaptive, intentional] system may be strongly influenced by the limits of its adaptive capacity." So strongly, in fact, that the eventual account of "economically rational" action must be tailored away from some notion of optimality and adjusted toward the account of the actual implementation of and methods for economic choice; the limits of the adaptive capacities of the system are central to explaining its behavior. Which is to say, if you like, that idealizing away from *breakdowns* in rational economic behavior is not at all the same as idealizing to some kind of *optimization*.

Unfortunately, the current situation in AI looks more like that of economics than that of thermodynamics. The distance between the task and process accounts will be great enough on an optimizing task theory that such a theory shouldn't be thought of as the proper idealization of the task that's being done. In cognitive theory, an optimization view at the computational or competence level will likely be an idealization that we may not even *approximate* in practice.[2] And the avoidance of an idealization to optimality requires a different application of the idea of boundedness than that which takes it as a kind of clarification of or variant on the idea of optimizing.

Boundedness needs to be seen not just as something that comes up in trying to *implement* a theory of cognition; its virtues vis-à-vis optimization should be made use of first from within the *task* perspective. Without doing so, the idealization to some kind of optimality beckons; and the overidealizations arising here will thus have direct and real consequences for theory-building. If the turn away from the idealization of optimality isn't made in the task account first, the task theory will mislead by suggesting that you focus on getting the system to do things it needn't do and putting off things that it should do.

Most importantly, the "boundedness as optimization" approach runs counter to some of the central needs that the generalized frame problem presents us with. As a variant of optimization, boundedness involves taking *more* information into account; but this leads away from a possible solution to the generalized frame problem, which requires us to *constrain* rather than *expand* the information considered. The need is to find a way to determine what is and isn't relevant, and what is and isn't worth spending time thinking about, and to make that determination *without thinking about it*—that is, without considering the irrelevant information to see whether it might be worth using. To do this means knowing when you've gone far enough; and this is the essential idea of a satisficing strategy. Without any such boundedness solution to the generalized frame problem, it will be in principle unsolvable.

---

2. Note that even the kind of guidance we can sometimes get from a decomposition of a complex system at a higher level of organization (discussed in chap. 1) isn't obviously forthcoming. But this question will resurface in chapters 7 and 8.

This may well underlie some of the critical problems involved in the use of "toy" domains and micro-worlds: By artificially limiting the domain and its taxonomic complexity, optimization may seem possible,[3] except for constraints on processing time, etc. But when you loosen the constraints that can just be built into the representation (since the restriction to the toy domain has guaranteed never needing to deal with their violation) and focus on real domains instead, the idea that *any* machine or algorithm could even approach optimization starts to seem highly implausible.[4]

Of course, this is the heart of the suggestion that "toy" domains "don't scale up." It's not just that these idealizations may grossly oversimplify the intrinsic degree of complexity in the real domain being abstractly simulated (e.g., as with the blocks-recognition idealization about spatial recognition) so as to lead to the adoption of strategies that will fail miserably when the simplifying assumptions of the idealization are loosened. It's also that an idealization that overshoots in the other direction—by an assumption of more ideally optimal behavior for either the overall system (as in the panglossian evolutionary case) or some of its components (as in the rational market agents of classical economics)—is equally prone to failure by missing the less optimal more contingent (and even chaotic) behaviors of the system.

5.4. Contingency and the Magic Algorithm

If what I've been saying is right, then the assumption of optimization in the idealized task theory of the mind would seem to place it beyond appropriate approximation by plausible accounts of realized procedural process. Such overidealization is the sort that in general undermines an idealization's power to accomplish one of its central purposes—the guidance of research attempting to provide an account of the underlying processing. Furthermore, it's not only—as Simon says about the domain of economic reasoning—that "the attainable approximate solutions to economic

---

3. Consider, for example, the classic idea [Winston 1975] of constraint propagation in blocks recognition where the domain has been constrained to where there are only 18 possible line junctions.

4. As Simon puts a similar point: "[The decision maker has] a choice between optimal decisions for an imaginary simplified world or decisions that are 'good enough,' that satisfice, for a world approximating the complex real one more closely" [1981a, p. 35].

decision problems are so far from the unattainable optimal solutions that we need to take account of the discrepancy between them in descriptive economics" [Simon 1981a, p. 36]. It's that we may be left without a general approach to idealized task *at all*—without any account of, in one sense, what the mind is *for*, or what counts as "right working." Without an idealization of this sort, we're left without any higher-level theory that allows the separation of what's *significant contribution to function* from what's *irrelevant noise* in the implementation—a position similar to that of sciences which suffer from the sorts of failings of overidealization mentioned earlier.

Without an appropriate idealized task theory of cognition, the study of the perhaps less systematic domain of human cognition might be seen as less like "science" and more like *engineering* than one might have thought: Rather than focusing on the discovery or systematic application of basic and general principles of cognition, the project may be more one of taking established inferential structures (be they Bayesian, non-monotonic deductive logic, case-based reasoning, or whatever) and finding out how to map the highly contingent structure of the information and inference with which human cognition deals—the structure which constitutes the human world we and our machines must physically and intellectually navigate.

To put the point another way: There is no "magic algorithm" for induction or solving the frame problem that we apply across domains and can potentially find so as to program it into the machines that we build. This is perhaps why AI is so much harder than people guessed at one time. Like the domains of economics, etc., we have in hand no idealized task theory to provide guidance in constructing our approximating algorithms. There may be no principled general science of cognition or epistemology as such to build AI toward or around. The path of inference, hunch, intuition, ignoring, and skill that we cut through the world may be a largely chaotic one in certain respects. We can't assume that there will be domain-general facts about us that dictate when a search for new information gets stopped or why one kind of taxonomy rather than another is used to generalize about a situation. The task of AI and Cognitive Science in general may well be more a matter of mapping a radically contingent epistemology for the world rather than to provide some sort of basic and fundamental algorithms (or "laws of thought") from which structure is to be derived.

The path not taken here is nicely illustrated by Stuart Russell's comments on the idea of "autonomy" (roughly, the independence of a system's behavior from the particular experiences and knowledge of its designer). The desideratum of autonomy is, for him, a very strong one; as he puts it, "a truly autonomous system should be able to operate successfully in any given universe, given sufficient time to adapt. A system's internal knowledge structures should therefore be constructable, in principle, from its experience of the world" [Russell 1989, p. 16].

It's surely exceeding unlikely that *we* are anything like truly autonomous in this sense. There may well be some sense in which "a system that operates on the basis of built-in assumptions will only operate successfully when those assumptions hold, and thus lack flexibility." But the flexibility lacked is a flexibility that *we* no doubt lack; and the flip side of the "lack of flexibility" is the entrenchment of patterns of processing that are attuned (in part through our evolutionary heritage) to the contingently actual structures worth picking out in the "blooming, buzzing confusion" of possible data faced in our environment.

We might quite naturally conceptualize the logic of the compromise on pre-programming in something like the following way: Pre-program to the extent that the costs of inflexibility don't overbalance the gains in computation that you get from that pre-programming. But this is an optimizing compromise. From the design view this is the optimal strategy. What changes when we insert boundedness into the design stance? What happens when the design point of view becomes a satisficing one as it must in the case of evolution or training? If what we're guided by is the existence proof of the possibility of rational behavior given by human rationality, we might naturally look at the process of design for those strategies. Of course, that means in our case looking at both the evolutionary process and the processes of training or learning which together produce our eventual strategies and patterns of bounded rationality. Evolutionary and training processes are, however, most naturally thought of as satisficing processes themselves. As Wimsatt [1986] has pointed out, adaptations fit all the central characteristics of *heuristics*. As such, many of their interesting properties will be determined not just by the task they arise to solve, but by the peculiarities and contingencies of their emergence.

Idealizing to the ability to in principle learn perfectly whatever the environment offers is another instance of just the sort of inappropriate overidealization that we've seen before. By setting this up as a guiding goal for the construction of an "autonomous" system, we aim at a task for which even rough approximation is intractable—but also, fortunately, a task that we needn't commit ourselves to. If *we* don't approximate such abilities, it's unreasonable to place that as a goal on the construction of intelligent machines.

Most centrally, I've suggested that the mistake of aiming for a certain kind of optimality—of taking satisficing as a variety of optimization—is to make the error of a kind of overidealization of the task (and thus of what the task account ought to provide). Overidealization to optimization can arise at the design stage; satisficing and boundedness are key parts of the task account to be used at the design stage, and not just aspects of the kinds of implementational limitations of process that Russell was getting at by calling satisficing "optimization modulo hardware." That idea makes boundedness into purely a process issue, while I'm suggesting boundedness as part of the nature of the task to be solved by the device. We should see boundedness as part of the sense of the logical task that's being solved—the task should be to accomplish some very bounded reasoning, and not something more optimal.

CHAPTER
S I X

EXPLOITING
THE
ENVIRONMENT

In chapter 2, I argued for the possibility of a non-individualistic view of the behavior of individuals; that is, for not *ruling out* an account of intelligent thought and action as essentially embedded. And in the last two chapters, I suggested ways that real cognition must be fundamentally bounded and that taking advantage of the contingencies of the environment would be an essential part of any successful strategy for a rational agent. In this chapter, I'll turn more explicitly to general kinds of strategies that a bounded rational agent might use to exploit the structure of the environment. In particular, I'll look at how such an agent might make very explicit use of the idea of redundant cues, multiple sources of information in the environment, and the contingent links between those and our abilities to detect them in finding appropriate strategies for dealing with its world. In doing this, I hope to begin to make more concrete the degree of intimacy between agent and environment involved in bounded cognition.

6.1. The Roles of Data

Nobody thinks that the environment is completely irrelevant to cognition; everyone allows that the mind interacts with the world in the sense that it gets *data* from the world and uses it. For example, I sample the visual array, see that there's an apple, and take the action of reaching out on the basis of that. But I'll want a notion of interactivity far stronger than this.

There are really two stronger notions to consider. The first, which I'll have far less to say about here, is the one that underlies notions of *learning*. Certainly the vast bulk of the information used in reasoning, recognizing, and so on originally comes from the structure of the world we confront. Even if you're disposed to make a fairly rigid distinction between the relatively fixed inference engine and the data in memory, the fundamental fact remains that we often act from what we've learned about the contingencies of our environment. Such information is sometimes treated as above—as "just" data, which is then operated on by the processes that are the real heart of intelligence. Theorizing also sometimes tries to avoid a deeper account of learning by focusing on explaining the abilities of mature, static devices, with a promissory note that the account of how there come to be such information-laden devices will be forthcoming once the problems of explaining the behavior of the relatively static systems are conquered.

In the long run, some account of learning will surely be a central part of an account of embedded thought and action. Interactivity is smoothed and enhanced in a multitude of obvious ways by allowing the device to mold itself to the contingencies of the environment it faces. Although the optimizing *tabula rasa* account discussed in chapter 5 is out, learning in general certainly isn't. We might for example, try to take advantage of something like a *case-based* account of reasoning, and carry some fairly detailed and structured episodic memory around to use as a guide to new situations.

I'll not go far down that path here. For one thing, the beginnings of such paths are already being traversed by others, and with more attention and detail than I can afford the issues here. But even more important, I think that a much more extreme notion of environmental dependence needs to be filled out. It's not just that you need interaction with the world to account for the structure that the organism comes to have in the process of learning; it's also that the processes of thought in the mature, tuned organism are processes that depend intrinsically on the structure of the environment outside the surface of the organism. If you can't even account for the structure of relatively mature, fixed and stable processes without central use of facts about the embeddedness of the organism, then you can't avoid considering the detailed character of the agent's interactivity with the contingencies of the environment by idealization to "mature" systems (where learning has mostly been done). The environment is then an ineliminable part of the account of thought and action even under the idealization of the organism as having completed whatever learning it does. For most of what follows, it will be this latter notion of embeddedness that I will focus on.

6.2. Effects of Interactivity

To begin, note that there will be no way to track behavior over any real duration without some appeal to the contingent structure of the environment. Consider two ways in which we might try to predict behavior: One would be to anticipate the trajectory of the body over time—to know the fairly fine-grained procedures which the agent goes through in the process of pursuing goals, etc. Such an account might include details like which way one turns on each step in a path, or even the pattern of the saccadic eye movements in searching for useful information. Alternatively, we might try to idealize away from such details and give a much coarser-grained analysis of the behaviors; not to taxonomize them in terms of bodily motions, but in terms of objects in the world that lump together a multiply realizable class of trajectories.[1]

The first of these could only be done (if at all) on the basis of an enormous amount of very detailed information about the structure of the environment confronted. When I go to the airport, which way my body moves has to do largely with the structure of the environment I meet along the way. I turn my head for horns; I move my hands on the steering wheel of the car one way rather than another because of what the last exit sign said; I push the brake or the gas pedal depending on the color of the traffic light in front of me; and so on, *ad infinitum*. Given appropriate motivation, it may well be a pretty good prediction that one way or another, come what may (more or less), I'll get there. But which of the uncountably many bodily trajectories I'll make along the way is a matter for me and the environment I confront along the way to work out between the two of us. It's these sorts of details of trajectory for which Simon's most radical conception of the interaction between organism and environment seems most compelling; i.e., that "the apparent complexity of his [i.e., the organism's] behavior over time is largely a reflection of the complexity of the environment in which he finds himself" [Simon 1981b, p. 65].

These fine-grained moment-to-moment fluctuations of thought and experience come from the world—they are, in some sense, "under the control of the stimulus." Against the background of the normal functioning of the organism, the particular contingent structure of the environment confronted is the central independent

1. See Pylyshyn [1984, chap. 1] for a discussion in this vein.

variable with which the fine-grained actions of the body fluctuate. Activity in this context is largely *reactive*. When we drive a car, much of the finer-grained structure of the complex path we take through traffic—when we stop, when we change lanes, etc.—is dictated by the contingencies of the driving environment. My behavior with respect to any given stop sign is relatively simple; while the *complex* pattern of stops and starts is a clear reflection of the complex pattern of the locations of such signs in the surrounding environment.

So even when I have a stable intention to get somewhere in particular (even by a particular route), the fine-grained fluctuations of perception dictate much of the moment-to-moment fluctuations in both behavior and the contents of consciousness And they must be explained in terms of their objects: The reason that I have one perceptual content to my thought now is that those particular objects are present to me. It's both the only way to predict these contents, and particularly the only way to predict and explain them *as perceptions of a certain content*—i.e., under the right description.

Some internalist motivations are entirely compatible with all this. It's a familiar line from the internalists that the level of rationality, intentional action, concepts, and reference is the (so far, one and only) level at which human action is systematic in such a way as to allow for the explanation of macro-grain behavior.[2] The purpose and guiding theme of giving intentional accounts of human action is surely to be able to explain why we do and think what we do; we must acknowledge that there will be very little ability to track consciousness, thought, and behavior over even the course of a few seconds without considering the ongoing flow of interactivity.

Above, I brought out how the fine-grained behavior of the embedded organism was fundamentally dependent on the contingent structure of the local environment faced. This is also true of more coarse-grained influences from the information in the world. More macro-grained behavior as well can be anticipated and explained only from the structure of the world and not from the structure of the organism in isolation. As in the kind of cases discussed in chapter 2—driving to Cleveland, wanting brisket—the information coming from the environment governs not just the fine-grained detail of the paths we take, but the more global shape of those paths—what we end up buying, where our bodies end up, and so on.

2. See, e.g., Pylyshyn [1984, chap. 1], and Fodor [1987b, chap. 1].

Both the macro- and micro-grained observations depend on the completely mundane observation that there is simply a lot of stuff that people will reliably realize and act on if they're appropriately situated, engaged in an appropriately related activity, and in a position to have their noses rubbed in it. Assumptions about the dependence of these regularities on those facts are typically not explicit in the structure of intentional cognition, but form the underlying background and underpinnings which are presupposed.

6.3. Control in the Environment

Recall that in chapter 2, one central aspect of the (rejected) idea of *methodological individualism* was that "the only mechanisms that *can* mediate environmental effects on the causal powers of mental states are neurological" [Fodor 1987a, p. 41]. At that time, I waved my hands in the direction of external mechanisms that might play critical roles in mediating behavior as well—social mechanisms playing the central role in the earlier discussion. Now I'd like to flesh that out a bit. What kinds of regularities and mechanisms outside the organism can mediate behavioral control, and how do they push some of the complexity of tasks out of the computational complexity of the organism and into the structure of the world?

Marr gives a particularly clean case of the exploitation of local environmental regularities in the control mechanisms of the common fly [Marr 1982, pp. 32–33]. Flies, it turns out, don't quite know that to fly they should flap their wings. They don't take off by sending some signal from the brain to the wings. Rather, there is a direct control link from the fly's *feet* to its wings such that when the feet cease to be in contact with a surface, the fly's wings begin to flap. To take off, the fly simply jumps, and then lets the signal from the feet trigger the wings.

This is a simple but clear example of how aspects of the local environment are exploited in the control structure for flight in the organism. Flight control depends not on signals from the brain to the wings. Instead, the fly exploits the environmental regularity provided by the surface (as well as its own sensory capacities) to run a part of its control loop *outside* its body and through its immediate surroundings. The local surface mediates the signal which, in a slightly roundabout but quite reliable way, makes its way from brain to wings. The fly beats its wings directly in response to a stimulus in the environment—the tactile change at its feet—but also consistently and reliably manipulates that stimulus so as to control flight from the brain as well.

Simon's ant [Simon 1981b] makes a similar point, but in a way that will bring out an important aspect of the interest-relativity of explanation here. Simon describes for us an ant, which in crawling across the sand of a wind and wave-molded beach, "moves ahead, angles to the right to ease his climb up a steep dunelet, detours around a pebble," and thus leaves a complex path behind it. As with the case of driving and dealing with stop signs discussed earlier, the complexity of the path becomes understandable only when we come to see it as the interaction of a simpler mechanism with a complex environmental structure—the uneven surface of the terrain. The ant "has a general sense of where home lies, but cannot foresee all the obstacles between" [Simon 1981b, p. 63]. As Simon puts it, "The apparent complexity of its behavior over time is largely a reflection of the complexity of the environment in which it finds itself" [Simon 1981b, p. 64].

In this case, it's quite tempting to think that we might also try breaking down the actions of the ant into basic and simple decisions about the next step or two made on the basis of the local terrain, and thus discover the procedures used by the ant to produce the complex behavior in interaction with the local data. There are two kinds of questions to ask here: One, what mechanisms internal to the ant contribute to the production of this complex path, and what are they like; and two, what is the explanation of *the complex path itself*—the eventual behavior? The first question is by definition one about the internal structure of the ant; but the second is, as a matter of contingent fact, one about an interactive process between organism and environment, and for which neither component alone could give the answer.

Which kind of answer is relevant depends on the kind of systematicity in behavior you are trying to explain. But as I've been pointing out, the answer in our own case is surely that at least some of the interesting systematicity is of the latter kind. The general starting point, which even the most rabid of internalists seem to agree on, is that it's the roughly rational behavior with respect to the world, our goals in it, and the general outlook of the intentional or rational level of thought that embodies the systematicities that are crying out for explanation. The questions now are: To what extent are those systematicities to be analyzed as due to complex interactive processes, where the role of the complexity of the environment is an ineliminable component? How do those interactions work? What aspects of the environment are critical and what strategies in the organism are central to taking advantage of them? I'll now turn to examining those questions more directly.

6.4. Reactivity

Another way to see the control of action as lying largely in the structure of the environment is to see action as largely *reactive*. Behaviors are reactive when their macro structure is determined by a series of reactions to more local conditions. Simon's ant-in-the-sand is a particularly good example of reactive behavior. The complexity of the ant's path is a consequence of the reactivity of the ant to the complex terrain it faces. It reacts to local convolutions of the terrain, and the complexity emerges. The fly discussed by Marr might also be seen in this light. The behavior of flapping the wings and thus flying is a reaction to the local conditions of having the feet off the ground.

Normal, coordinated bodily actions are also good illustrations of reactivity. In the standard hand-grasping problem, we face the delicate and complicated task of deciding exactly how far to move our arm, hand, and fingers, and where to place them so as to grasp the cup in front of us; holding it firmly enough that it doesn't fall, but not so firmly that we cause damage to it. In such cases, we take advantage of significant tactile feedback from the cup to feel its position in our hand, how likely it is to slip, and the amount of pressure we need to place on it, as well as tactile, visual, and proprioceptive feedback to determine whether the hand has yet touched the cup.

In these cases of reactivity, the macro goal is explicit, but the local details of the strategy are determined by reaction to the feedback acquired during the activity. This might be contrasted with the similar notion of *opportunism*. Where reactivity focuses on the *implementation* of processes where the macro goal is explicit in the organism but the local strategy is not, opportunism is a way to take advantage of the dynamic and unpredictable environment by letting it cue the activation of explicit goals. So, for example, you take advantage of the opportunity to get milk, because you're at the store, you need milk, and seeing the milk at the store reminds you of the goal to get milk. Opportunism might then be thought of as most centrally a matter of *reminding*; of allowing the environment to trigger and activate goals which the agent already has [see Hammond 1991].

6.5. Enforcement

The idea that every action and every passage of time will bring about changes in the environment because of the dynamic nature of the domains in which we operate is one that played a critical role in our discussion of the frame problem and boundedness earlier. But not all of our environment is in constant flux and change; much of it is stable. Inanimate objects stay in place, people have the same names from one day to the next, and money doesn't disappear from your wallet without a little help.

I have largely focused on ways in which we might exploit situations in the world that we find to accomplish cognitive tasks and maintain consistency. But we might also *enforce* on the environment certain kinds of stable properties that will lessen our computational burdens and demands on us for inference. As Hammond puts it, "Fixed location for objects reduces the need for inference and enables the execution of plans tuned to particular environments. If your drinking glasses are all kept in one cupboard, you can get a drink of water without ever considering the real pre-condition to the plan that they are in there now" [Hammond 1990, p. 204].

We not only enforce this kind of stability on the environment, we also often enforce a structure on the environment to reduce load in other ways—as, for example, when we set the local world up so as to remind us of various things. We put the gas gauge in the car where we'll notice it; we put the letters by the door so we won't forget to mail them; and leave the milk sitting on the counter where we'll see it and remember to put in back in the refrigerator. Further down the same path, we write things down to read later, or record them in a computer to be presented or recalled later. Using the locally manipulatable but stable structures of the world, we manage to increase the effective capacity of our own available long-term memory.

This allows for a natural blurring of what should count as part of our memory and what should be counted as part of the external environment. When asked if I know the phone number of a particular acquaintance, it's in fact not entirely clear whether the answer should be "yes" or "no" if I know it's on this list in my wallet but can't recall it off the top of my head. Conventionally, we probably say something like "yes, just a minute"—in the same way we might if asked to calculate a sum, or remember what we had for breakfast. In terms of the *macro*-grain behaviors we exhibit, this is clearly about the best answer available. The information available to us in deciding what to do, and even what we know, is not so clearly circumscribed at the boundary of the physical organism. In much the way we naturally idealize to an expectation that people will act on what they have in long-term memory, we naturally idealize to the use of external facts which are under normal circumstances just as accessible and immediate. If you know the facts about the world (like that there is a huge clock on the wall) and something about interests (like that this place has valuable scheduled appointments, and that is why folks are here) then you should assume that everybody is roughly in direct contact with what time it is, regardless of what the microstructure of their thought is when they enter the room.

Simon gives an interesting twist on this idea: His notion of the embedding of the agent counts our long-term memory as a part of the *environment*. As mentioned earlier, Simon's radical way of putting the suggestion of the intrinsic embeddedness of human intelligence is to say that "A man, viewed as a behaving system, is quite simple. The apparent complexity of his behavior over time is largely a reflection of the complexity of the environment in which he finds himself" [Simon 1981b, p. 65]. But even he sees this as overstating the point, and qualifies the point by suggesting that " . . . a human being can store away in memory a great furniture of information that can be evoked by appropriate stimuli. Hence I would like to view this information-packed memory less as part of the organism than as part of the environment to which it adapts" [Simon 1981b, p. 65]. And although I still find this a bit strong (as I'll discuss later), there is a clear and important point: From the point of view of information, the interesting distinction is not the organism/world one, but something more like the inference engine vs. the database; and the database includes both things inside the organism like long-term memory, but also things outside the organism, including the structure of both the social and the local physical world.

Structure is also enforced *socially* on the environment. There are lots of obvious ways in which the *social* embedding of information in the world allows us to use local and bounded strategies to be nonetheless sensitive to quite distal information. An enormous amount of the informational structure of society is set up just so as to allow us to have access to parts of the world that are important and interesting to us but don't happen to be right there to see. All kinds of signs fulfill this function, and in particular, the signs of linguistic behavior. To make use of facts that lie outside my immediate perceptual range, I can take advantage of the fact that there is a rough convention of reference and truth-telling and ask somebody, or make use of the fact that it's Burger King signs that are to be reliably found near Burger Kings rather than Texaco signs, and so on. It may be really hard to guess whether there's meat over the next hill in the natural environment; but it gets lots easier once the "butcher" signs are up in the supermarket.

6.6. The Virtues of Procrastination

Throughout chapters 4 and 5 the central underlying suggestion was to think less by exploiting the information in the world more. Another way to view this suggestion is as advocating a kind of strategy of *procrastination*. Never do today what you can put off until tomorrow. Think as little as you can at any given point; (whenever possible) use the heuristic of "I'll cross that bridge when I get to it." This heuristic for planning and acting can obviously lead to problems at points—as when we paint ourselves into corners. But there is a tradeoff between considerations of painting yourself into a corner and the benefits to be gained by a strategy of procrastination.

Historically, the emphasis in planning and problem-solving in artificial intelligence has gone the other direction. The overall strategy has been to avoid painting oneself into a corner at all costs. Planning a complex activity is seen as essentially the process of providing a proof that a certain procedure to accomplish that activity would succeed. This strategy, typically known as *classical planning*, emphasizes decidability ahead of time over ability to react, improvise, and back out of failure gracefully.

But it has become commonplace to notice that classical planning seems entirely intractable in domains with significant complexity, dynamic structure, uncertainty, or interactivity between the actions of the agent and the eventual outcome. This has led to the emergence of a more embedded perspective in AI. The contrast with the classical model is put nicely by Agre and Chapman in one of the seminal papers in this trend: "Before and beneath any activity of plan-following, life is a continual improvisation, a matter of deciding what to do *now* based on how the world is *now*" [Agre and Chapman 1987].

The emphasis in traditional planning on having well-specified plans prior to acting places critical value avoidance of failure, and on avoiding situations that require backing and filling. That's a worthwhile goal; but it's important to trade it off against the benefits of procrastination. Focusing on both the dynamic indeterminacy of the environment and the possibility of exploiting rich and redundant cues in that environment (see below) emphasizes the degree to which *anticipation* may be costly and perhaps in the end not a productive bounded strategy.

The connections to the problems of overidealization we considered in chapter 5 should be clear: Trying to approximate ideally rational behavior (where we *don't* make mistakes and then need to backtrack and correct) may be just the kind of misguiding idealization we need to worry about. If we end up idealizing to strategies where we *never* paint ourselves into corners (even corners we might be able to back out of gracefully), we've focused away from virtues of a strategy that trades more mistakes for the benefits offered by the embedding of cognition in its dynamic and rich environment. A strategy of more procrastination will fail under some conditions. But substantial reliance on such a strategy might still be a critical part of our bounded intelligence.

A key theme of chapters 4 and 5 was the importance of strategies for *implicit ignoring*. What kinds of general constraints should such strategies try to meet? One is fairly straightforward and trivial: Ignore something if it just won't matter at all—that is, it won't be linked to *anything* that I care about. So, for example, there's (fortunately) no connection between the Cubs' record and the fluctuations of the stock market; so I should just not consider that possible connection. But another guiding principle is even more at the heart of the more embedded conception of cognition: Ignore things which will *eventually* arise and require that we deal with them, but where procrastination will bring real benefits.

Rather than making a detailed plan about the directions and moves I'll make in running the kickoff back in a football game, I can take a general and momentary guess, and then allow the new information about the developing situation in front of me (which is clearly far too indeterminate and dynamic to predict) to help me make those decisions. I reduce the space of possibilities by putting off the decision, and I get new information that allows that decision to be made more easily. I cross bridges when I get to them; and I find out that I need to cross when my feet get wet. In short, we often take advantage of one of the world's somewhat trivial but amazingly useful properties: when you most need information about some part of it, that part might well turn up. It's no accident—it's often the stuff *around* that we both had better care about and that it's easiest to find out about. The nearby dangers are typically the ones it's most critical to avoid, and the local food is the first choice (as it costs little in uncertainties and exertions).

We might separate two distinct benefits of this kind of procrastination. First, there's much indeterminacy that's resolved in dynamic environments. Rather than trying to predict particular states of the environment that are highly dynamic (and thus from the agent's point of view, either very costly or just impossible to predict), *procrastinate* in the hope that the prediction that would have been costly won't after all be needed. Don't spend too much time wondering what Number 63 is going to do in defending against your run; with lots of other defenders out there, the chances are that he won't be the critical factor anyway; put the work off until the world forces you to face it. By doing so, you may in fact get in the position where he causes you problems that you could have in principle anticipated and avoided, if you'd thought about it hard enough. But the strategy is one of making the right overall bets for thinking about the right things. Ignore it for now if, on balance, the expected value of knowing it is outweighed by the costs of in general thinking about it.[3]

Second, and perhaps more important, there's the virtue of procrastination that comes because the information that you'll get later is often richer and allows for taking advantage of more easily exploitable cues not available until the last minute. This may well then make the problem more tractable by dealing with things when they come up, and not before. This strategy will be expanded in the next section.

So we can potentially gain in efficiency and reduce computational overhead by (1) letting the world tell us when to worry about it, and (2) taking advantage of further and more detailed information available in the later situation. These are the central cases for

---

3. In line with chapter 5, this principle needn't be used in execution by the device at all, but is simply a desideratum from the design perspective.

filling out a more *reactive* or *improvisational* account of thought and action.

6.7. The Uses of Redundancy

Another key feature of embedded cognition is the exploitation of *redundant cues in the environment*. We often can take advantage of re-parsing a complex environment to find a taxonomy of the complexity that allows the key features for action to be more directly taken from the environment, with less effort—i.e., finding a simpler parsing of the environment from the point of view of the agent's skills and abilities. This re-carving of the environment in order to exploit the rich information in it—common now to many discussants in the AI literature—might be summarized as the strategy of exploiting the *redundancy of cues* available in complex environments.

As Chapman nicely puts a part of this idea, "toy" domains are *"too hard because they are too simple"* [Chapman 1990, p. 1]. When information in a toy domain is pre-distilled, the high degree of redundancy available in real environments is removed, thus making strategies that focus on getting the right information out of the complexity pointless. So, for example the "simplification" of studying activity in isolation from perception makes the problem harder, not easier, because the richness of perception may provide alternative categorizations of the domain which might greatly simplify the kinds of heuristics that can be used to provide constrained but implementable real-time solutions.

So in vision, distilling a visual display to a 2-D line drawing before trying to figure out the 3-D structure of the scene removes some of the kinds of rich complexity that might in the normal case make this task much easier. I can in the real case use information from my own motion, stereopsis, and so on, to decode the shape of a corner in 3-D, rather than having to use the propagation of physical constraints through a fixed 2-D diagram. I actually can figure out corner orientations locally, by directly perceiving their 3-D structure via parallax caused by my own motion, my binocular vision, and so on. Or in language: By distilling language to a stream of characters, I remove the cues that are normally available in stress and intonation. But recovering the intent of the question "Why did Adam eat the apple?" is made significantly easier by the extra richness of stress.

By hearing "Why did *Adam* eat the apple?" I can figure out that you mean to ask why *Adam* (rather than *Eve*), as opposed to asking why Adam *ate* it (rather than, say, smashing it).

A key point in chapter 1 is surfacing here: the idea that central to analyzing a complex system is finding the right strategy for distillation of the complexity, which will determine which aspects of the activity are central and basic. This will play a key role throughout the discussion of the next several chapters. Reconceptualizing which aspects of the complexity of our activity are the significant and systematic ones and which are noise is central to the reconceptualization of cognition I'm advocating. Intonation in speech above shouldn't be distilled out as noise, nor should motion of the organism and the object in vision, the pragmatic skill of identifying the referent of a demonstrative (see chap. 8) and so on.

Another central point so far has been that strategies for real problem-solving must make strong (if still implicit) use of assumptions about our strengths and weaknesses in gathering and using information. And one natural way to do that is to avoid the costs of maintaining a rich model of a highly dynamic environment by relying less on prediction and modeling and more on perception. "Letting the world be its own model" means that you have to focus on the interface to the environment rather than the maintenance of a more complex internal model. We trade complexity of modeling against speed, reliability, and flexibility in perception. We can take a strategy of waiting longer and looking more; but to do so, you'd better be able to quickly and reliably read the right kinds of properties off the perceptual environment. In doing this, you might fail to be clever and flexible enough to get *useful* properties off the local environment—ones that correlate enough with what you really want to know about that the trade-off is worthwhile. If the decoding task takes you too much work, avoiding inference is no gain. So how do you get the benefits of boundedness from the system that emphasizes perception over modeling?

Consider the problem of keeping track of the myriad of objects swarming around as you move through an assortment of objects—some with independent movements of their own to track. You might create an internal model of the local scene, and then as you move with respect to it, calculate the new scene from some geometry (in the way, say, a video game does). But if your head isn't very good at this, then you likely will and should take advantage of the fact that you already have access to a model of the environment that is *really* accurate—*the environment itself*—and just look again and see what it looks like from the new angle. It's a worthwhile strategy if you've already got a really good device for reading the environment, and keeps the load on model maintenance down.

If you're going to the store, how do you figure out that you need milk? Not by counting the number of gallons you got last time, the amount you've drunk since then, and subtracting; but just by looking in the refrigerator. It's a handy correlation that the amount of milk you see when you open the refrigerator is a terrific indicator of how much you actually have. We also often take advantage of pre-structured parts of the environment, and that some more easily detected parts of the environment are good indicators of some less easily detected parts. Much of this kind of correlation is a part of the natural structure of the physical world (as with the link between how the milk bottles look and how soon I'll need milk). But much will also be part of the socially structured world: In the most general case, I learn to take advantage of correlations between what people say and what the state of the world is. In general, we "cheat" off correlations between the easily-parsed properties of the environment and the ones that we care about for action.[4]

Notice that this idea of the exploitation of the redundancy of information in the environment fits nicely with the discussion of robustness and distal causation at the end of chapter 3. As in the earlier illustrations of distal causation (where the causal link between the distal object and the local state is more explanatorily central than the—possibly multiple—intervening causal routes), the exploitation of the redundancy of cues suggests a process dedicated toward decoding aspects of the *distal* environment by taking advantage of whatever possible cues might turn up—i.e., by having multiple and redundant cues for the presence of various kinds of objects in the world. We allow that the path between a distal object and internal state might be highly different in different cases, but that the underlying systematicity is the systematicity between object and agent.

4. We might again appeal to a kind of design-stance decision-theoretic perspective: Making use of contingent environmental cues will be worthwhile just in case by doing so we save more time and effort than we would lose on average given the probability of those cues leading us astray and the lost utility of those cues leading us astray.

6.8. Situated Cues

Although re-parsing to use cue redundancy is an important aspect of the exploitation of the richness of the environment, it's not the only one. Perhaps even more important is the context-sensitivity and situatedness of strategies for action, identification of objects, and so on.

In a given context or situation, the amount of information needed to interact usefully with the *local* environment is dramatically constrained with respect to the amount and kind of information that you might need initially to identify the situation and the objects in it. Once I've determined that you and I are alone in a room, I can simply pick you out as the large moving object in the room—a task that may take far less work and information than continually re-establishing that as my gaze comes back to meet you again, it's still *you*. Once I make those determinations, I can take advantage of constraints in the particular local context and track you with a less globally detailed check on your identity. Or I might (as I'll discuss in more detail in the next chapter) link local objects with a rough color histogram for them and use that to re-identify them in the local context—in spite of the fact that the rough histogram might not even come close to picking that object out uniquely in other contexts [Swain and Ballard 1992].

A similar theme crops up in speech perception. What acoustic pattern counts as a phoneme of a particular type is highly dependent on the surrounding speech context [Nusbaum and DeGroot 1991].

Not only is this the case for general feature of context (e.g., the phoneme produced by a given acoustic signal is contingent on, say, what vowel it precedes), but the overall context of a particular speaker and utterance can change to boundaries for phonemes. So in *vowel normalization*, we adjust our perceptual space for vowels to the different carvings of it done by individual speakers. What counts as an "a" in the context of one speaker may count as an "e" for that of another.[5] Or, consider that the substantial variations in speed of speech (even for a given speaker) can change the relevant context, so that what will count as a phoneme of a particular type can vary along with the speed of speech. So, for example, the difference between /ba/ and /wa/ is a difference in voice onset time.

---

5. See the end of chapter 7 for more on this.

The surrounding speech can make the same local acoustic pattern an implementation of /ba/ rather than /wa/; i.e., there are acoustic patterns that occur in rapid speech and instantiate the /wa/ consonant but occur also in slower speech and there instead implement the /ba/ consonant [Miller 1981]. These features are a central part of what makes speech-to-text processing so hard, particularly across different speakers.

But to look at this from another angle, once the speed context is fixed, or once the vowel space is normalized to a speaker, the task gets significantly simplified. Indicators which aren't in principle or perfectly generally indicators of whether a /ba/ or a /wa/ was uttered become entirely good indicators in context.

In all these kinds of cases, what we see is a central interaction between *redundancy* in the available cues, and *context-dependence*. The cues for a particular phoneme, or the position of a particular person, are various and redundant. We might detect them through different means; we might have a strategy that provides necessary and sufficient conditions for being that phoneme or that person in that position. I take advantage of the fact that in the highly situated context, there is a cue that picks out you specifically, even though that exact same cue might pick out all sorts of other people in other contexts. We can take advantage of the stabilities in the world—even fairly temporary and local ones—to restrict to amount of information we need to use in any particular contextual setting.

Using these features of redundancy and context-dependence of cues together will be a central part of the general account of using embeddedness to facilitate effective bounded strategies. In the next part of the book, I'll turn to more concretely making use of these features in various domains.

PART THREE

Minds in the World

CHAPTER SEVEN

INTERACTIVE DECOMPOSITION

T hrough the last three chapters, I emphasized some of the constraints and opportunities that present themselves to an agent (or device) trying to make its way in a complex and dynamic world. I offered some motivations for finding an approach to the relationship between cognition and world that emphasizes the fit and interactivity between the two. In so doing, I focused on the importance of finding strategies for constraining search, inference, and computation by taking advantage of information offered by the environment to lessen computational burdens. And in chapter 6 in particular, I laid out some of the more general structures of interactivity as a foundation for embedded cognition and action.

In the current chapter and the next two, I'll try to make more concrete some strategies for exploiting embeddedness and achieving effective bounded rationality in real agents in a real world by showing how the current perspective fits with some recent puzzles and progress in the study of intelligent behavior. In each case, I'll go through some illustrations of how we exploit the environment's structure in accomplishing the intelligent behaviors in our repertoire, and also suggest a re-interpretation of some common views about the relationship of thought and environment and the role of the organism/environment distinction.

Starting in this chapter, I'll look at the possibilities for the decomposition of an agent's information-processing structure. By considering the give-and-take between the decomposition of the task faced and the processes that might be used to accomplish it, I'll try to shed light on some of the motivations and reservations concerning aspects of the decomposability and possible *modularity* of the system. In doing this, I hope to offer a perspective on decomposition which will both capture the virtues and avoid the pitfalls of more standard and well-known accounts of modularity and decomposition—in part by taking advantage of some tactics available to embedded systems.

Then in chapter 8, I'll discuss the relationship of this approach to recent work in the philosophy of language. I'll try to show how contemporary trends in the philosophy of language—particularly the "new" or "causal" theory of reference and meaning—comprise some of the most explicit shifting toward an embedded account of cognition. And in chapter 9, I'll turn to perception, and consider how the current approach can help make sense of an important germ of truth in the suggestion that perception is in some sense "direct."

7.1. Boundedness and Encapsulation

The general idea of the higher-level decomposition of a complex system that I've been using throughout is naturally taken as suggesting some kind of *modularity* of higher-level components—or, as Herbert Simon originally put it, the *near-decomposability* of components of complex systems. In considering the behavior of some functional component in a system, you'll typically focus on facts about the subsystem's overall behavior with respect to its inputs and outputs relative to the rest of the system. For example, an arithmetic subroutine doesn't care why it's been asked to compute $24 + 17$ instead of $98 - 56$; what matters for analyzing the complex system that contains the subroutine is that it accomplishes those arithmetical tasks given to it. It is, in most respects, indifferent to anything else going on in the system; it's largely *modular* or *encapsulated*. Simon's original notion of the near-decomposability of complex systems is stated in terms of the strength of linkage between components. As he puts it, a system is nearly decomposable if intercomponent links are sufficiently stronger than intracomponent links.

Assumptions of modularity are motivated in a variety of ways; two will be particularly important here: The first is that modularity provides a kind of *distillation* strategy (see chap. 1) for the explanation of complex systems. There is an obvious appeal to a kind of divide-and-conquer strategy for complex systems. Defining subsystems whose behavior in relative isolation is similar enough to their behavior in the real, embedded context, we might hope to come to understand the complex working of a system piece-by-piece. The trick, of course, is finding out when systems approximate their normal behavior in isolation; and it's assumptions about this kind of approximation that often turn out to be the soft underbelly of assumptions of modularity.[1] And the second central motivation for looking toward modular subsystems is as a route to providing a certain kind of bounding on inference and process—in the way discussed in chapters 4 and 5. Modularity of processes is quite naturally seen as motivated by certain kinds of satisficing or boundedness tradeoffs.

Informational encapsulation for any decision is a way to accomplish a bounding strategy: Constrain what can influence that process—i.e., what that process has access to—and you thereby constrain both the ideal rationality of the process (given that ideally, anything you know should be able to bear on an inference) and also how much the process has to do. Trade the virtues of encapsulation against the drawbacks of limiting information.[2] Dramatically limiting the information available to the module has the drawback that there will be information that the organism has straightforward access to that the modules won't listen to—as in the case of, say, the persistence of illusion. The appearance that the two lines are different lengths in the Müller-Lyer illusion does not go away even though I know that they are of different lengths; and similarly for the other well-known stable illusions.

The reliance on these sorts of "stupid" bounded modules has a particularly effective role within the framework of embedded cognition. Such bounded modules might be attuned to properties of the environment that are more easily detected by such bounded systems, but which are also contingently correlated with the properties of the environment that we are interested in. This way of exploiting the redundancy of cues is the way discussed in chapter 6.

The use of color vision is a good example of this. Primates, who don't synthesize vitamin C, take advantage of the correlation in the environment between the foods they eat (which contain vitamin C—fruits) and their color (bright colors like reds and oranges, typically) to detect those foods. By gearing the detection apparatus

1. See Fodor on "The first law of the non-existence of cognitive science, that is, the assertion that the more global a cognitive process is, the less anybody understands it" [1983, p. 107].

2. As Fodor [1987b] puts it, there is no frame problem for the modules because they constrain the database for inference and search *a priori*. But note that he also places significant restrictions on "bottom-up" flow *from* modules to "central systems." The reasons for this are less obvious, given the unbounded nature of central systems on his view.

to colors rather than some more hidden but directly relevant property of the object, you give up some reliability—e.g., you might mistake flowers for oranges occasionally—for a huge gain in the cost-effectiveness of the search. You use mechanisms that can fairly directly detect the colors of objects, but not ones that distally detect their vitamin C content. (And as noted in chap. 6, we set up much of our social world to establish such exploitable correlations in order to ease the burdens of getting around—e.g., as with street signs.)

The use of these contingencies again illustrates the exploitation of a kind of mismatch between task and process. The task of finding foods containing vitamin C in the local environment is accomplished by a process defined over the colors of the objects. This contingent correlation allows real simplification of the process of search, while the correlation insures that in the normal environment, this process does after all provide a solution to the task confronted.

The flexibility and potential usefulness of such strategies can be broadened dramatically by allowing for periodic and temporary "tuning" through some restricted top-down information flow to such constrained subsystems. This provides a further elaboration of the notion of "situated cuing" discussed in chapter 6. In a local context, easily detected properties of the environment will, over some at least short period of time, correlate nicely with more complicated properties of the distal environment. By tuning modules locally to those properties, we get detectors for properties like being a person, and so on, which would have been far more difficult to detect themselves; by allowing small adjustments in the tuning of the modules, we let the less-powerful subsystems locally do a job that they could not do globally. So top-down flow of information is needed to allow for a kind of guiding of modules on this approach.

7.2. How Much Encapsulation?

But the well-known modular accounts of both Marr and Fodor explicitly appeal to fairly dramatic limits on top-down information flow. Marr, who places the boundary of the visual module overall at the point defined by the representation he calls the "2-1/2 D sketch," insists that up to that point, "the processes can be influenced little or not at all by higher-order considerations" [Marr 1982, p. 351]. And as Fodor puts it, "the operations of input systems are in certain respects unaffected by [higher-level] feedback" [Fodor 1983, p. 65].[3] What underlies this restriction, and why?

The observations about boundedness in modules above are certainly in keeping with the spirit of fairly standard motivations for modularity.[4] But the mistake lies in moving from these observations to a particular kind of distillation strategy for decomposition of the cognitive apparatus, in which we postulate "perceptual mechanisms . . . which compute the structure of a percept largely, perhaps solely, in isolation from background information" [Fodor 1983, p. 66]. Marr makes this methodological strategy for distillation quite explicit. As he puts it for the case of vision, "[if] we can experimentally isolate a process and show that it can still work well, then it cannot require complex interaction with other parts of vision and can therefore be understood relatively well on its own." [Marr 1982, p. 101].

Seeing modules as "ignoring lots of the facts" or as being best seen as independent of interaction with the rest of the system is being motivated in these cases by a sense of constraints on the kinds of processes at work. If the process is seen as one of one of "checking the facts," we'd better ignore a lot of opportunities to do that to get real-world performance. But there may well be routes to "checking the facts" which don't bring on this informational explosion—a suggestion I'll fill out below.

And Marr's suggestion runs together the idea that such an isolable subsystem cannot *require* complex interactions with other parts, with the suggestion that it can therefore "be understood relatively well on its own"—i.e., that the basic and fundamental process should be seen as the isolated one. But the former does not at all entail the latter. The subsystem might, for example, still roughly accomplish its task under highly informationally impoverished conditions, but might do so in a way that's not a good indication of its normal pattern of working. For example,

3. Fodor in fact pays explicit allegiance to Marr's views here, claiming that "my impulse in all this is precisely analogous to what Marr and Poggio say motivates their work on vision" [1983, p. 73].

4. See, e.g., Fodor's "prima facie reasons for doubting that the computation that input systems perform could have anything like unlimited access to high-level expectations or beliefs" [1983, p. 66], and his suggestion that "speed is purchased for input systems by permitting them to ignore lots of the facts" [p. 70].

it might work longer and resort to less efficient means to solve a problem than it would under conditions of normal informational access do quickly, effortlessly, and automatically. The case of isolation would then give a misleading view of how the process works. The fact that we can recognize animals purely on the basis their gaits [Todd 1983] or faces purely from line drawings of them should not indicate that the best understanding of the normal process sees it as operating only on this kind of constrained information.[5]

To reconcile the virtues of boundedness with those of top-down information flow to perceptual modules, we just need a different model of the process which will require neither a blanket restriction against top-down flow nor a sophisticated meta-reasoning strategy on the module's part for constraining its own search. Instead, we need a way to make the amount and kind of background information available to the module *not something that is under its control*. The module needn't control its own search, but might consider everything it has. The control on the degree and kind of background information may come from the outside systems which prime the module. The correct task account then allows that the module be sensitive to—or if you like, penetrated by—all sorts of background information. But the process is such that the control of which information is available comes from outside.

Marr and Fodor offer essentially the same reason for strongly restricting top-down information flow—roughly, that without such restrictions, the prospects for progress are dim. Marr says that an approach like his would be likely to fail with "systems that are not modular . . . that is to say, complex interactive systems with many influences that cannot be neglected" [Marr 1982, p. 356]. And as Fodor puts the claim, "the limits of modularity are also likely to be the limits of what we are going to be able to understand about the mind . . . [because] the condition for successful science (in physics, by the way, as well as psychology) is that nature should have joints to carve it at: relatively simple subsystems which can be artificially isolated, and which behave in isolation in something like the way that they behave *in situ*" [Fodor 1983, pp. 126–127].

---

5. This kind of distillation move engages in what Wimsatt [1986, p. 301] calls the "localization fallacy"—the bias to "look for an intrasystematic mechanism rather than an intersystemic one to explain a systematic property, or if both are available, regard the former as 'more fundamental' ".

7.3. Access and Control

Fortunately, the kind of restriction against top-down flow of information suggested by both Fodor and Marr is actually not well-motivated. Information coming from outside the module does not necessarily impugn the virtue of the module with respect to the avoidance of the frame problem. To see this, we need to be more careful about distinguishing between potential *routes of information flow* in the system and the structure of *control of process*. This is another use of the task/process distinction; this time helps separate the notions of *decomposability* or *modularity* from that of *informational (im)penetrability*. In making use of modularity as a boundedness heuristic, it's important to see that modularity as *decomposability* is a *process* notion, but modularity as *informational encapsulation* is a *task* notion. Or if you prefer: Informational penetration is an informational or semantic notion, while *decomposability* or *modularity* (or in the sense I want, *access*) are *process* notions.

On the surface, the idea of a module's *access* and its *penetrability* from outside are really just the same—both are characterizations of constraints on information flow *into* the module from the outside. But there is a difference: The penetrability of a module suggests the *insertion* of information by outside action, as when we vision an explicit instruction for interpreting a degraded display as a particular kind of object (see chap. 9). On the other hand, we might think of the *access* of the module as being under *its own* control. It searches for and gets some information.

The critical difference between these two ways of seeing the access is in what determines the *control* structure of the process—or if you prefer, where the *strategy* for access and ignoring comes from. In speaking of the module's access, the control structure is determined by the module; in speaking of its penetrability, the control is determined from outside.

Priming, for example, can have systematic effects on various recognition tasks—e.g., seeing "nurse" immediately prior to the "doctor" will speed up the recognition of "doctor" as a word (as compared to, say, "bread"). [See, for example, Meyer and Schevanevelt 1971.] Such priming effects are generally quite transitory and fleeting. Similar effects can be gotten through hints and prompts. We recognize the object (see fig. 9.1 in chap. 9) after we're told it's there. Perhaps we explicitly feed the visual system with some hypothesis. Cooper and Shepard might be taken as suggesting this:

Reaction times for determining whether the second of two visual presentations of a letter is the same as or a mirror-image of the first are slowed by rotating the second presentation of the symbol into a non-upright position. But the slowing disappears if the subject is informed ahead of time as to the rotated orientation that the second object would be presented in. Providing time prior to the presentation of the second stimulus (allowing for internal rotation) was critical for achieving the facilitation [Cooper and Shepard 1973].

And in speech recognition, Stanovitch and West [1983] have given a detailed look at the influence of congruous and incongruous context on recognition of words given as the completion of a sentence. Compared to concluding words which are neutral with respect to the context, congruous context facilitates recognition immediately; but incongruous context inhibits recognition only when a delay is introduced between the context and the target. Facilitation by congruous context might well be done by direct activation links in the lexicon; but inhibition by incongruous context will more likely require deciphering and feeding back more complex combinatorial aspects of the sentence.

In such "prompting" cases, perceptual processing might seem to be getting some input from elsewhere in the cognitive system. But receiving such input doesn't mean that the process isn't still some largely isolated component in the system. In addition to the proximal representation of stimuli, you can have one extra input— the internal prime. But all the perceptual system has access to is the representation of the proximal stimulus, the representation it's primed with, and its own internal rules and information. The process might be local and encapsulated in terms of which particular representations it takes as input, but still be sensitive to (and so not encapsulated from) almost any information in the system—at least, any that could affect which representation is used to prime vision.

A locally encapsulated mechanism—with access only to some constrained class of inputs and their shapes—might then still be indirectly sensitive to essentially any information in the system in which the local mechanism is embedded. Even if as *process*, the subsystem only sees local syntactic properties of its own constrained set of inputs, it can still be sensitive to the information carried by those inputs. Locality of mechanism, near decomposability, and all those desiderata are compatible with the penetrability of the subsystem by any information you like. The modularity of process of a subsystem is a matter of which syntactically specified inputs it is sensitive to—which inputs, which representations, whatever. But its information encapsulation depends on whether that information can, *via some route or other*, get into the subsystem and influence its operation.[6]

Modules need to have their access restricted in order to be bounded, but the restrictions on their informational penetrability are far less obvious. They might be penetrable to all sorts of information without their effectiveness as bounded devices being impugned. The concern for using encapsulation as a strategy for boundedness is centrally one about whether *processing* is localized. And encapsulation shouldn't require that the behavior of a subsystem be independent of the content of the representations of other domains. Modularity requires that the module be sensitive directly only to the local, syntactic, and descriptive properties of the representation that it sees.

We can see not how top-down effects can actually accomplish *greater* boundedness rather than destroying the encapsulated bounded inference in the modular processor. The top-down influence can serve to focus processing towards certain possibilities, thus speeding the recognition of those possibilities. In the cases of sentence completion where top-down contextual effects actually do predict the eventual stimuli, processing in the module is actually more bounded, more constrained, and requires the devotion of less computational resource. It's done faster, and the lexical search process is generally less costly.

The top-down context *might* misdirect lexical search and slow it down. A kind of bet is being made—a bet on context, a bet on the high-close ending for a sentence. If the bet pays off, computational resources are saved. It's not top-down flow into the module that destroys boundedness. Unrestricted search by the module into additional contextual information would destroy boundedness; but constrained top-down flow makes just the kind of satisficing bet for computational payoff that has been typical of highly-bounded processes.

6. Note how experimental situations often dodge some of these complexities by allowing for a "practice period" which can allow for this tuning and thus get past the active top-down direction of the module. This might well allow subsystems to approximate real encapsulation in the experimental setting, thus falsely downplaying the importance of a kind of guided encapsulation that depends on some fine-tuning in a given type of task.

The critical point to note about the examples here is that they allow informational *penetrability* of the module without allowing *unrestricted informational access* by the module. The modular system can be given a second input, if you like, by top-down information flow, but this input can be used in the same control structure simply to target the processes. Whether the search then becomes more bounded (as in a lexical recognition task) is a matter of the detail of the task and its answer. If the targeting is effective, as when we get top-down anticipations for the high-close ending which then actually occurs, the additional information constrains rather than expands the search and the devotion of resources.

7.4. Components and Skills

I think that the considerations I've reviewed so far point us in a particular kind of direction in looking for patterns of decomposition in the cognitive system. In the tug-of-war between modularity and holism, the equilibrium point may well be a type of building block exhibiting a kind of limited modularity which allows it to capture the most natural set of strengths. Such a type of subsystem gains significant support for its suitability to exploiting the virtues of embeddedness.

The kind of fundamental components that I'll consider here— largely encapsulated systems which still allow for top-down information flow and short-term tuning—have a fair bit of affinity with what might have more traditionally been called *skills*. And although I don't have any wish to rest much on whether this is the right thing to call a skill, in the end, the congruence with aspects of skill that have been pointed out by others is striking enough that it's worth pursuing a bit.

As Dreyfus puts it, bodily skills "are not something we *know* but . . . form the way that we *are*" [Dreyfus 1982, p. 21]. They are aspects of our intelligent activity which, as Chomsky [1980] puts it, are a matter of "knowing how" rather than "knowing that." Their essence is in the behavioral ability, and not in the logical structure of the processes that produce it. They are activated by the external context, and are not very available to introspection or detailed intervention. Consciously accessible rules or procedures may well play a role in the learning of a skill, but they don't seem to do so once that skill has been thoroughly learned. When we learn a dance, we seem to cease to be conscious of the procedures (e.g., "first move the right foot back, then the left foot in . . .) we used in learning.[7]

The skill-like building blocks discussed here share a number of interesting properties. We might expect to find significant modularity for the kinds of reasons considered earlier in this chapter; but we should also be particularly attuned to mapping inter-modular information flow—and especially the possibilities for targeting the search by subsystems so as to (heuristically at least) reduce their burdens. By dealing with specific domains of activity, such systems might also use more proprietary representations of the features of the domains. This fits naturally with the idea of re-taxonomizing the complexity of a domain so as to become more optimized or tuned to the contingent correlations in the environment. As noted above, the use of such redundant "secondary" cues can facilitate real performance.

And such correlations needn't be fixed; the exploitation of only temporarily stable "situated" redundancies in cues may be in the end even more critical. Top-down flow of information can—as noted earlier—allow us to take advantage of such situated cues. To get the taxonomy you want from the local environment with "stupid" (and thus maybe *modular*) processes may often mean tuning the modules a bit to the current context where you can take advantage of local correlations (e.g., of a given vowel triggering a certain physical resonator). That is to say: Use dumb but situatedly accurate techniques. Short-term tuning allows bounded and automatic modules to be retuned to a new taxonomic space of stimuli by temporarily focusing more and other resources on the problem, re-carving the space, and then pulling those resources back and leaving the dumb and automatic module to do the job. This way we get the re-parsing of the complexity on the basis of locally useful cues (even if they aren't in general the most accurate ones).

So we can take advantage of constraints in the particular local context to simplify the cues needed to re-identify objects. This interplay between *redundancy* and *context-dependence* in cues can be effectively used by such short-term-tunable modules. Temporary adjustment of mostly encapsulated subsystems is a mechanism for accomplishing the kind of situated tuning discussed in chapter 6. By temporarily refocusing the processes being used and so tailoring

7. See [Fitts and Posner 1967] for a nice discussion of this kind of skill learning from within the cognitivistic framework.

our search to the context, we use the situation not only to drive the search for different cues, but also to change the way we evaluate the cues we do use in order to enhance the likelihood of a faster search for an answer. So in vision, for example, we might take advantage of the color histograms presented by local objects to re-identify them in the local space. Even a fairly rough color characterization of the local objects will typically discriminate them from each other, in spite of the fact that a vague color histogram will hardly uniquely identify the objects in general [see Swain and Ballard 1992].

This all in turn allows for various ways in which we might rely on exploiting the regularities in the environment. The processes underlying our skills will often be complex and interactive ones, in which key positions are taken by highly particular and contingent external variables, and are such that the disturbance of those variables can cause dramatic erosion of the abilities. Changing the inertial feedback into the vestibular sense will dramatically impair our abilities to ride bicycles or navigate crowded rooms; and changing the distribution of weight in the ball will have serious consequence for our ability to shoot it into the basket. And of course, the case is even worse for regularities we might think of as being less basic and more structural. Change the naming convention about streets, and my skills at navigation will deteriorate in a hurry; change the contingent relations between the sounds made by a speaker and the appearance of his/her face, and my ability to understand speech will suffer [Massaro and Cohen 1983]. These links can create dependencies on aspects of the environment which may not have seemed initially critical to the task. For example, when I play basketball, I have a very hard time with my "post-up" play (i.e., playing with the ball but with ones back to the basket) when I play on an unmarked or incorrectly marked surface. Clearly part of the skill of playing the post-up relies on getting cues about my position from the markings on the floor. I never consciously try to; I just do.

A fair degree of micro-scale automaticity and modularity here also can encourage allowing the macro structure of more complex behaviors to be determined by a series of interactions with more local conditions—that is, they encourage *reactivity*. A clear illustration of this is given by the standard hand-grasping problem considered in chapter 6 (where we face the task of adjusting the movements of our arm, hand, and fingers, in order to grasp an object with the appropriate amount of pressure so as to neither drop nor crush it).

Rapid and automatic adjustment to tactile, visual, and proprioceptive feedback allows the structure of the task to dictate the detail of movement without significant attentive intervention or detailed pre-planning.

We are again "letting the world be its own model"—or more descriptively, we make direct use of the world *as it responds to our bodily activity*. As in the case of running the kick back in football, I make local and short-term decisions, avoid over-anticipation, and continually sample the changing local environment.

By using local cues and exploiting the structure of the environment without necessarily internally representing that structure, we can manage to accomplish the complex and systematic tasks without systematically representing the task structure as such, and thus creating a kind of mismatch between the task and the process. The description of *task* systematicities will typically be in terms of external objects, in terms of parts of the surrounding environment, in terms of achieving certain goals such as moving to a place, capturing a certain creature, reaching a certain object, and so on.

The systematicity of *process*, however, will typically be more fine-grained, and will look more at local properties of the environment. To illustrate: When we have a route of deliveries to make, the systematic task structure is one of getting to all the possible locations. The process structure will entail the reading of local traffic markers, the handling of the car, and so on. It is a more micro-level process, and it is also one where the match in the end between the behavior it generates and the satisfaction of the task constraints depends in a very detailed way on the kind of information coming from the environment in the execution of the process, and the kinds of information used may be only contingently linked with the goals that we have in the way that the street signs are contingently linked with locations.

7.5. Concrete Application

Tasks in speech perception show many of these features. One such task is that of *vowel normalization*—the adjustment of our carving up of the acoustic space for vowels to the patterns of different speakers. Here we see both long- and short-term tuning of the organism: we learn to taxonomize the vowel space grossly in our language, but we also tune in a short-term contextual way to the vowel space presented to us by an individual speaker. This takes additional attention for a moment, but allows for less cost afterwards in sorting out which vowel is being spoken. We may well use highly modular processes to detect the speech, but guide them with some initial attention in order to tune the modular process to the particular taxonomy needed for the current speaker; after which we can allow it to go on about its business detecting the complexity and taxonomizing it. And we let the world be its own model in that we don't carry around a representation of the vowel space for every person all the time, but we just pick one up and re-tune to it each time.[8]

The task of decoding the complex speech stream into the vowels is one that's done not in some single way; rather, there is a fundamental difference between the first second or so and later on. The process is first one of computationally expensive retuning, and second, one of simplified detection on the basis of that retuning. The process then is one which has a kind of complication that the task does not. And we see a change in the kind of distillation that we do in order to shift the noise significance line. We see the variance between individuals as significant now, rather than just noise. It's a significant part of seeing how the overall task grows, allowing for it and allowing for the initially computationally expensive task of tuning into the new speaker. We then allow ourselves to use more simple strategies for decoding the vowel space after the first second—ones which would give significant wrong answers if we just used them without the initial tuning period.

A similar kind of account can be given of various features of vision—something I'll return to in more detail in chapter 9. We see here both short-term and long-term tuning in that we can train the visual module over the course of development to decode certain kinds of shapes, and short-term tuning surfaces in cases like those of priming phenomena. We see significant modularity, but with guidance as well—not only in the priming cases, but also in the task-sensitivity of the continuous and rapid retargeting of the variable-resolution sensors (the eyes). And as I'll emphasize in chapter 9, we re-parse complexity as distal layout, and let the world be its own model in our using constant scanning in place of main-

---

8. A kind of enforcement occurs in that we actually also enforce our own vowel space on the environment—that is, the local social environment of listeners. It's been suggested [see Nusbaum and DeGroot 1991] that typical noises of greeting actually serve this function better than one might expect from random speech sequences.

taining a complete high-resolution picture of the distal layout. And by moving from "picture" vision to *animate* vision, we change distillation strategies and thus redraw the noise/significance distinction so that the constant movement and varying resolution of the visual field now becomes a significant part of the data that indicates to us a different way of carving up the complexity.

But I'm getting ahead of myself. Language first, then vision.

EMBEDDED LANGUAGE

I n the last chapter, I worked up to the point of considering how social factors in thinking, planning, and acting play an impor- tant role. In particular, I began to consider how the social use of representation might play a critical role in allowing the organism to exploit the structure of the environment without having to store and manipulate too much information itself. Clearly shared language is a kind of public representation that carries an enormous amount of information about the environment and allows us to take advan- tage of the information provided by other agents around us. We can exploit this information because we know what the utterances we encounter *mean*. In this chapter, I'll consider how the knowl- edge underlying our exploitation of meaning might fit in with the embedded epistemology I've been advocating. Not surprisingly, I think the fit is quite good.

My central point will be that the traditional notion of meaning[1] as something cognitively grasped, as something "in the head," is fundamentally an epistemological notion; and the epistemology it depends on is the one that I've suggested we should leave behind. There has been emerging over the last forty years or so a different conception of knowledge of language, stemming perhaps most cen- trally from Quine and Wittgenstein. This notion of language use and knowledge accords much better with the embedded epistemology I've been advocating, and gives us part of an account of embedded language which forms a critical part of the overall picture.

Before continuing, let me emphasize that I'm not going to try to give here any particular non-internalist account of meaning. Com- ing up with a theory of change of meaning, sameness of meaning,

---

1. This is often characterized as the "Fregean" notion, although the historical accuracy of this ascription is in some question—Frege may or may not have been what we now call a *Fregean* [see, for example, Burge 1979b]. In what follows, I'll use "Fregean" in the now-conventional way; but I don't mean to assume anything in particular about the views of Frege. Treat the words as homonyms, if you like.

communication, and the like is a difficult project on any account of meaning—and no less so the externalist one. What I would like to do is to provide a theory schema for the overall structure of the knowledge of meaning, of the structure of our abilities to manipulate language, behave systematically with respect to it, and so on. How much distance there is between any account of meaning as the bearer of truth-value (if one is to be found) and an account of the knowledge underlying the meaningful use of language of the sort I'll point to is something I won't prejudge here. It's entirely compatible with the morals of chapter 1 (and, I think, the rest of this book) that an account of intentional content be largely autonomous with respect to the account of the skills underlying it—in much the way one might have thought that an account of the structure of language (or grammar) might have been given independently of an account of language learning. The project of unification or complete dissociation I leave for another time and, I hope, for another author.

Probably no area of philosophy has undergone more dramatic change during the last thirty years than the philosophy of language. The conventional wisdom for at least the first half of this century was, very generally put, logical empiricist. What Quine [1953] labeled the "two dogmas" of empiricism were at its heart: The fundamental cleavage between analytic and synthetic truths, and the reducibility of the meanings of terms to some kind of "direct experience." The reference of words was taken as determined by the meaning, intension, or sense associated with them; and to understand a word or to know its meaning—to "grasp" its sense, in the "Fregean" way of speaking—was to know some kind of definition for it in terms of something like a logical construction from primitive sense-data.

Let me start out with a little historical narrative about how the philosophy of language got to where I think it is now. This will be a bit of a "just so" story—my "just so" story about the emergence of embeddedness in the philosophy of language as it comes up in a particular kind of issue of meaning and reference. I intend this only as a summary of what has come so far; I won't be trying to *make* the now-standard arguments, but comment on where they might have left us.[2] In fact, I think that the recent philosophy of

2. Of course, chapter 2 offers an argument which I think makes a contribution to this debate in and of itself.

language has offered some of the greatest progress toward a more embedded conception of epistemology so far. So in this section, I'll summarize some of that progress; and then turn in the next section to offering a positive extension of what I see as (what I'll characterize as) the largely negative morals of the movements in the philosophy of language.

8.1. A "Just So" Story about Meaning

Once upon a time, there was a distinction called the "analytic/synthetic" distinction. It separated off into fundamentally distinct classes the *analytic* truths—those true simply in virtue of the meanings of the terms in them, as with "bachelors are unmarried men"—and the *synthetic* ones—those true in virtue of some fact about the world itself, such as "There are nine planets." It was a big, powerful distinction; the philosophers made it, and they saw that it was good. Maybe every once in a while there would be rumblings from the other side of the English Channel from the phenomenologists; but that was well-known to be meaningless metaphysics anyway. All us good upright Anglo-Americans knew that the analytic/synthetic distinction was the basis of all clear thinking—not to mention giving the philosophers a domain to work on (that of the analytic truths) where they didn't have to know anything that everybody didn't know already. Never mind that the positivistic project of finding the (analytic) definitions of terms by some kind of logical or conceptual analysis, or by giving observational criteria for the application of terms, hadn't been going so well—in fact, it hadn't come up with a single case where it had done well. Still, it was an article of faith that this could be done, and was immediately obvious to anyone who bothered to think about it for more than a moment or two.

Then along came big, bad, Willard Quine. In "Two Dogmas of Empiricism" [Quine 1953], he pushed the issue of the possibility of giving up on the analytic/synthetic distinction into the heart of analytic philosophy. Quine's two dogmas lay at the heart of the traditional conception of meaning: the idea that there was a fundamental cleavage between the *analytic* and *synthetic* truths, and that the mundane terms in our language had definitions in terms of some kind of semantic primitives—typically, raw-sense data, or some other notion of direct experience. *Definitions* (which were of course analytic truths) were central to meaning: Knowing the meaning of a term was a matter of knowing the correct analytic truths which defined the term via a logical construction from the semantic primitives (e.g., the sense-data). Or to put it more generally: To know the meaning of a term was to know the necessary and sufficient conditions for its correct application.

But our apparent inability to find definitions for terms—and in particular, definitions given in terms of any circumscribed class of semantic primitives—had become annoying at best. By codifying the general principles which apparently were underlying this conception of language use, Quine did as much as anyone to suggest that they may not be either justified or unavoidable.

The traditional view has crumbled. First it suffered at the hands of Quine and the Wittgensteinians. But then—more importantly, I believe—it buckled under the challenges posed by the theories of reference and meaning often dubbed "causal," which stemmed largely from the writings of Hilary Putnam and Saul Kripke in the late 60's and early 70's—particularly Putnam's "Is Semantics Possible" [Putnam 1970] and "The Meaning of Meaning" [Putnam 1975], and Kripke's *Naming and Necessity* [Kripke 1980]. On this new conventional wisdom, the meaning of a term is not taken to be fixed entirely by some associated cognitive structure (e.g., a *definition* of the term that the speaker knows). Rather, it's taken to depend most centrally on what it is *in the world* that the term *refers* to. Reference, in turn, is then fixed primarily by some kind of causal, historical, or social link to the referent itself. Rather than seeing reference as a function of meaning, the new theory give reference a kind of priority.

The aspect of the move from the old to the new account of reference and meaning most central to the current discussion is the degree to which the shift was both motivated by and helped bring about a shift in perspective toward seeing meaning as *nonindividualistic*. Perhaps the most recognizable slogan of the new account of meaning is that—as Putnam put it—"meanings just ain't in the head" [Putnam 1975, p. 227]. On the traditional account, the *meaning* or *sense* of a term had at least two roles (perhaps three—see below) to play: that of being the feature of the term that fixes what it's about (i.e., fixes its *reference*), and that of being roughly *what you know* when you know what a term means (the term's *cognitive significance*). The central suggestion of the new theory is that *whatever* conceptual connections you make in knowing what a term means, that isn't all there is to fixing the term's referent. Something else about the (external) context of *use* is critical—perhaps facts about the physical structure of the world, perhaps facts about the social context.

This point has often been illustrated by the now infamous "Twin Earth" examples in philosophy [see Putnam 1975]. In these, we imagine some world like ours in almost every respect (including the internal states of the world's human-like inhabitants); but different in just such a way that—although the internal states of the people aren't affected—our intuitions about the reference of various words and thoughts are. Make the stuff that comes out of faucets have a different chemical structure, and their word "water" refers to *that* stuff rather than H_2O [Putnam 1975]; make their physicians use "arthritis" differently, and the reference of those of us less well informed about the details shifts too [Burge 1979a]. The physical and social world may determine a concept's reference and boundaries as much as the form of our internal representation of those concepts.

One nicely evocative way of putting this general point is given by Putnam in "Brains and Behavior" [Putnam 1963]. The new conception of language calls for separating our metaphysics from our epistemology. We should separate the idea of *what we know* when we know the meaning of a term and how to use it from *what it is that determines what the term is about or refers to*. As Putnam points out, diseases are not logical constructs out of the symptoms they produce. What makes a disease an instance of *polio* is that it shares an important etiology with cases of polio, not that it necessarily produces exactly the same symptoms. *How you tell* whether something is an *F* or not and *what makes it the case* that something is an *F* have thus been torn asunder. There is no more central idea in the general conception of the new theory of meaning and reference.

8.2. Stop Making Sense

In his paper, "Frege on Demonstratives," John Perry [1977] nicely summarizes a kind of disintegration of the traditional (or "Fregean") account of meaning. As he points out, Fregean sense has three very distinct roles to play: *cognitive significance*, the *fixation of reference*, and *reference in indirect quotation*. Above, I noted that the separation of the first two of these is perhaps the most central theme of recent philosophy of language.

The notion of "cognitive significance" that's appealed to here is a fundamentally "solipsistic" one; that is, type identity of cognitive state ought to be guaranteed at least by physical type identity of subjects.[3] More simply: cognitive state ought to be a characterization of our psychological subject itself, and should be in some sense indifferent to what goes on outside the subject. The breaking of the connection between this notion of "psychological state" and the fixation of reference in recent philosophy of language has been the focus of much of this chapter so far.

As for separating individualistic cognitive significance from the ascription of propositional attitudes, Burge's "Individualism and the Mental" [Burge 1979a] is perhaps as central a piece as any. Burge points out that the normal practice of ascribing propositional attitudes depends at least in part on relationships that the subject of the attitude-ascription has toward states of the world. To put it in a way more common to the philosophy of language, even *de dicto* attitudes have some significant *de re* component. The pre-theoretical individuation of propositional attitudes often individuates them as relations to the states of affairs or even objects in the world.[4]

In the case of the explicitly indexical expressions, like the true demonstratives ("that," "this," "he," "she," and so on), this observation is mundane and ubiquitous. To ascribe the attitude to John that he would ascribe by saying "*I* lost the game," I need to use the expression "*He* lost the game." I shift what Kaplan [1989] calls the *character* of the demonstrative in order to preserve the same *content* (which for indexicals, is essentially *reference*) in the case of such explicit indexical expressions. Even Fodor, perhaps the most rabid defender of a methodologically solipsistic view of propositional attitudes in the end will admit, " . . . there are nevertheless some [external] semantic conditions on opaque type identification . . . . [T]he notion of same mental state that we get from a theory which honors the formality condition is related to, but not identical to, the notion of the same mental state that unreconstructed intuition provides for opaque construals" [Fodor 1980, p. 67]. There will be case of both "formally distinct" thoughts with the same content— e.g., explicitly indexical cases: my thinking "I'm sick" your thinking "he's sick" are "thoughts of the same (opaque) type (and hence of the same content) . . . " [Fodor 1980, p. 67]—and formally identical

---

3. See Fodor's discussion of this in chapter 2.
4. Again, see chapter 2 for more detail.

thoughts with different contents—e.g., as in the standard sorts of "Twin Earth" cases discussed in chapter 2.

David Kaplan gives a "two-tiered" story about the meaning of indexicals to account for this shift. For Kaplan, the *character* of an expression (indexical or not) is to be thought of as something like the cognitive significance of the expression; "as *meaning* in the sense of what is known by the competent language user" [Kaplan 1989, p. 505]. But Kaplan's *content* is to be equated with "what was said" via a particular utterance in a particular context; it's the sort of thing that determines reference and truth-value.[5]

Once you've made a content/character distinction for indexical expressions, it's quite tempting to reapply this distinction in order to generate "narrow content" for terms other than the indexicals. But there are two reasons why this is a mistaken strategy. One I'll turn to later is that once something like the content/character split is made, we notice that there isn't in fact anything that plays the role of character—that is, any single thing that should be reified as the character of an expression. The underlying cognitive or epistemic significance of a term is just too varied, multiply realized, and context-dependent to be reified as some single thing.

The other is brought out by Burge in "Other Bodies" [Burge 1982]. Burge's central point here is that the kind of context-dependence of meaning and reference exhibited by natural-kind terms—or even just the explicitly non-indexical terms—should not be subsumed to the context-dependence of the explicit indexicals because of a fundamental difference in the way the context-dependence functions. Burge argues that "there is no appropriate sense in which natural kind terms like 'water' are indexical," and that hence, there is no "convenient and natural way of segregating those features of propositional attitudes that derive from the nature of a person's social and physical context, on the one hand, from those features that derive from the organism's nature, and palpable effects of the environment on it, on the other" [Burge 1982, p. 103].

As Burge points out, indexicals are (at least) terms that "have an extension which varies from context to context or token to token." But the *natural* (and *social*—see below) *kind* terms don't have this

---

5. It's actually what we are to hold fixed when, through the use of modal and intensional operators, we want to evaluate what someone said with respect to some counterfactual situation.

property at all. As he says, "water, *interpreted as it is in English,* or as we English speakers standardly interpret it, does not shift extension from context to context in this way" [Burge 1982, p. 103]. The analysis of natural kinds as indexical:

> is no more plausible than saying that 'bachelor' is indexical because it means 'whatever social role the speaker applies "bachelor" to' where 'the speaker' is allowed to shift in its application to speakers of different linguistic communities according to context . . . . One must, of course, hold the language, or linguistic construal, fixed. Otherwise, every word will trivially count as indexical. For by the very conventionality of language, we can always imagine some context in which our word—word form— has a different extension . . . . If Indians applied 'bachelor' to all and only male hogs, it would not follow that 'bachelor' as it is used in English is indexical. [Burge 1982, pp. 103–105]

The insight of Burge and others has been to force us to see the ubiquitousness of such effects of features that do not supervene on the local structure of the speaker, and how they effect not just indexicals. Beliefs about water are not simply a matter of the character of a particular kind of expression, but about it being related to a certain stuff, H_2O, in a certain way. And contemporary work in the philosophy of language has extended this moral to cases where the non-individualistic constraints on meaning and reference would seem to be social rather than natural, as in the case of "brisket" discussed here in chapter 2.[6]

8.3. A Last "Grasp": Narrow Content

"Grasping" the sense of a term is perhaps the most central traditional metaphor for understanding or knowing the meaning of a term. Fodor's "formality condition" is one way to try to cash out something like the notion of the cognitive significance of a term—the thing which on the Fregean model is "grasped" when we understand a term. It's this notion of cognitive significance or the "grasping" of sense that I'm going to focus on here. Definitions which provide necessary and sufficient conditions for the application of a term are one clear way to try to fill in an individualistic epistemic notion of sense. But the psychological and epistemic implausibility of such a notion of definition—along with the split from

6. The canonical version of this is Burge's "arthritis" case [see Burge 1979a].

reference fixation and propositional attitude content—has largely discredited such an approach.

One response to the disintegration of Fregean sense has been to try to construct a notion of *narrow* sense from what we have. We might acknowledge that the single notion of Fregean sense is breaking down, and take the role of sense in psychological explanation— in taxonomizing the states of organisms so that we can engage in psychological explanation—as the most critical. We might insist then that we should search for a clarified notion of sense that plays at least the role of the old one in subsuming interesting systematicities in our behavior. We commit to finding some notion of cognitive significance that's roughly the same as the one we started with, but strips out all the non-individualistic features.

Unfortunately, this seems typically to be motivated not so much by its natural or interesting explanatory value, but by the assumption on metaphysical or methodological grounds that there *must* be *some* such notion. This "narrow content" move is of course Fodor's line [Fodor 1987b], and it's the one I rejected in chapter 2. There, I argued that the constraint of a kind of "methodological solipsism" on our psychological taxonomy is not to be inferred from any obvious prior principles about explanation in psychology or sciences more generally. The current trifurcation of sense (following Perry) gives another way to see the claims of chapter 2: The non-individualistic component of propositional attitude ascription is not to be glossed away from when you move back to cognitive significance, if the point of cognitive significance is to capture intentional generalization. That notion—as I suggested earlier—is embedded and non-individualistic.

The problems here start to look like a very characteristic failing of philosophically motivated methodological outlooks. As I mentioned at the end of chapter 2: "preferences" under conditions of dramatically constrained contextual information, behavioristic "responses" to linguistic items isolated from any kind of context, and over-idealization in classical economic theory all seem to be cases where a methodology generated by mistaken epistemic or metaphysical views has been allowed to ride roughshod over critical facts about a domain. As Neisser [1976] put it, we too often fail to make the appropriate "commitment to the study of variables which are ecologically important rather than those which are easily manageable" [Neisser 1976, p. 7]. We have been looking for our lost keys under the lamppost because that's where the light is good.

8.4. Knowing How to Refer

On a positivistic or pre-Quinean account, there is a nice, clean epistemology of meaning, where meaning is reduced to "semantic primitives"—like sense-data—through some kind of logical analysis. Knowing the meaning is then knowing the appropriate analytic truths that reduce more mundane expression to logical constructions out of sense-data; more generally, it requires knowing necessary and sufficient conditions for the ideal application of the term. And this traditional account was right about one thing: Knowing what a term means is roughly knowing how to tell whether something is one. Or in a more Wittgensteinian tone: It's knowing how to *use* it, where the part of use that's important is knowing when it applies to something and when it doesn't (as opposed to that part of use that tells you, say, whether that's a polite word to use).

But what the traditional view was wrong about was the epistemological account of what "knowing how" should look like. Traditionally, knowing *how* has been subsumed to knowing *that* by the analytic philosophers. Knowing how to tell whether something is a *P* is a matter of knowing something like the necessary and sufficient conditions for being a *P*. The traditional account of meaning can be seen as collapsing the task/process distinction in a misleading way; and knowledge of meaning should be taken as more a matter of what I have called a *task* rather than a *process* account. Accounting for meaning in terms of necessary and sufficient conditions for the application of a term (and knowledge of meaning as knowing those conditions) runs together *what counts as* appropriate application of the term with knowing the meaning of the term. That is, it runs together the idea of the *task* of application itself, with that of the *process* by which we accomplish that task.

The tendency to see knowledge of meaning as something like knowledge of necessary and sufficient conditions for a term's application is an interesting kind of overidealization, much like that looked at in chapter 5. Even once we see knowing meanings as some kind of *task* rather than *process* story, we've overidealized about the conditions under which the substantive rationality or competence holds. We fail to allow for highly contingent and context-dependent strategies for picking out the reference of terms. By not allowing those on a more traditional account, we're left to look for an account of how we might be able to pick out the appropriate referent in all possible contexts. Hence the account of meaning as cashed out in terms of "reference in all possible worlds." The mechanism by which we might do anything like that must be something like knowing the necessary and sufficient conditions for correct application. Overidealization about the account of the task to be dealt with has led us to an unrealistic account of the procedural theory that underlies that competence.

The perspective of embedded cognition and the separation between the task and process accounts that it helps to emphasize can cast a significantly different light on how we think about the epistemology of meaning—one that shares far more with a kind of Wittgensteinian idea of *meaning as use* than it does with the traditional account of having necessary and sufficient conditions for a term's application. Knowing the meaning of something isn't being in some particular privileged mental state, but it's instead being able to use the term right—which is to say, how to (in some sense) *find* the referent.

But the ability to get to the referent is a great example of something like a *skill*, as discussed in the previous chapter. Like the paradigms of skill noted there, the essence is in the behavioral ability, and not in the logical structure of the process underlying it. The abilities are facilitated by and highly dependent on details of the external contingent regularities in the environment—the markings on the floor in the basketball shooting example discussed in the last chapter, the regularities in the use of language by the other members of language community in the case at hand. Like the earlier examples, much of the detail of skill in meaningful language use are relatively impenetrable to our introspection. As Dreyfus put it, such skills "are not something we *know* but . . . form the way we *are*" [Dreyfus 1982, p. 21]. They are less propositional structure than form of life.

Reconsider the "brisket" and "Cleveland" examples discussed in chapter 2 in light of what's been said here. In each case, what's critical to the use of the expression in ascribing an intentional state to the subject is not that it picks out some particular associated description or "narrow content." Rather, it's that it presupposes a particular kind of ability on the part of the subject—in each case, the ability to pick out the object in the world, which is a matter of having intentional behavior that's systematically related to that object or class, however the route to the object might be mediated. In the case of driving to Cleveland, the skills will typically take advantage of road signs, abilities to maneuver a car, to ask directions, and so on; for brisket, one might take advantage of the social skills needed to negotiate the process of labeling a transaction in the delicatessen. In each case, the skills are making use of kinds of social indicators of the referent, rather than relying on the richness of some internal symbol representation or conceptual framework.

It's no accident that it's *proper names* for which the New theory of reference was largely developed. Kripke, in *Naming and Necessity*, focuses first and foremost on proper names, as terms for which there is no associated description that specifies their meaning. And Kaplan, in *On Demonstratives*, takes proper names as the paradigmatic case for which content and character collapse together—the determination of both being what he calls a "pre-linguistic task." These are of course the cases for which the intuition seems clearest that competent use means basically being able to pick out the referent; and the ways in which we might go about picking out the reference could be dramatically varied—through social or historical link to them, through perceptual recognition, and so on. In fact, picking out the typical objects for proper names—*persons*— by perceptual recognition is a particularly nice case to notice here: There is perhaps no domain in which our abilities to discriminate and recognize so far outstrip our abilities to describe—no domain for which in which "a picture is worth a thousand words" is more appropriate.

So we take advantage of our own perceptual skills in many cases where those skills and their deliverances have no distinctive conceptual decomposition for us—like when we recognize particular people. This is one way to take advantage of the indexicality of language to make finer-grained linguistic distinctions than we have on the basis of "conceptual" distinctions alone. Part of what specifies that meaning of a demonstrative—even on a mainstream "Fregean" account like Kaplan's—is a "completing character" provided by an associated demonstration. We use ostension rather than conceptual description to provide the filled-out meanings of our expressions in this way.

We also take advantage of the linguistic division of labor rather than trying to carry with us a strategy that would allow us ideally to separate the world into the parts that fall under a particular concept and those that don't. We use the skills had by others in our society for doing so.

One obvious way in which this is done is by taking advantage of the knowledge of experts in a domain. We needn't understand exactly the difference between beech trees and elm trees, if we can consult botanists, encyclopedias, or gardeners. When in doubt we take advantage of the knowledge of language use had by of domain experts—those who have specialized knowledge of the area where the term applies. But this is not the only way that we take the advantage of the knowledge of others to establish reference and concept boundaries. On a much smaller scale, we often take advantage of the deictic reference of others in particular discourse context to establish reference to an object that we're far from being able to pick out uniquely by providing some description of it. Discourse-level anaphora is probably the clearest case of this; but the use of proper names where we don't know enough to fix the particular reference is also a clear case. We allow ourselves terms that refer without our being able to cash out the referent, without our being able to provide necessary and sufficient conditions for the application of the term in the context.

8.5. Pragmatics and *Sinn*

Recall that the most explicit point of Frege's "On Sense and Reference" [1980] was to give an account of how co-referential expressions could differ in cognitive significance or, as Frege put it, "how identities between co-referential expressions could be informative". From the very start the notion of Fregean *sinn* was a notion of cognitive significance and an epistemic notion.

A way to take the suggestion that runs through this chapter is that "sense" is no such thing—there is no cognitive significance notion of sense to be found. That notion of "sense" is an epistemological one; and our epistemology has changed enough that we now should realize that there *is no such construct* to be used as a central notion in epistemology. The informativeness or cognitive significance of an expression is so loaded up with pragmatic considerations (background that we bring to the understanding contextual effects and so on) that to make "sense" a single entity preserved across all of these cases is to make a mistake. This is of course the standard problem of *meaning holism* faced by any conceptual-role based account of the semantics of psychological states. It's been with conceptual-role based account since Field's seminal "Logic, Meaning, and Conceptual Role," and is acknowledged by Fodor—one of the most dedicated advocates of "narrow" content—to be the most serious problem for any such view.

At least one notion of meaning of the three that Perry isolated for us should be discharged. The internalist conception of meaning "sense," cognitive significance, and the like, is to be left behind in favor of, if you like, an *existential* semantics, which unavoidably depends on situatedness in the world where in a certain interesting sense *existence precedes essence*. Of course one way to cash that out is to paraphrase it as *deixis precedes description*. Our pragmatically grounded abilities to pick out objects in context through our embedded activity allows our abilities in determining *deictic* reference to far outstrip our abilities to determine reference "purely descriptively"—on the model of the old "sense-grasping" view.

The shift from meaning as necessary and sufficient conditions to meaning as *use* allows a reconceptualization from something like *semantics* to *pragmatics*. As some kind of fixed cognitive value to be associated with an expression has now gone by the wayside, the cognitive value of an expression is instead to be associated with a complex and shifting class of skills, background knowledge, abilities to exploit social structure, strategies for locating objects, contextual features of discourse, and other kinds of pragmatic considerations. If the knowledge of the meanings of terms in your language is essentially a knowledge of something like the conditions of appropriate use, the pragmatic features of use no longer need to be "second-class" criteria.

All this has a natural fit with the "redundancy of cues" account given of embedded cognition in chapter 5 and then filled out in chapters 6 and 7. The idea that we exploit highly redundant information to take advantage of what's salient and easy to get from the world in constructing our actions and plans encourages us to think that there is no privileged form or source for the information used. When we know how to apply a term, we make use of whatever there might be. What's critical is that we get to the referent; and whether the facts, guesses, skills, and strategies used are definitional or pragmatic ceases to seem important. The exploitation of redundancy of cues available in the environment that's been a central theme in the last few chapters again seems to play a central theme in the account of the knowledge of language as skill that's been pointed to in this chapter.

8.6. Distillation and Activity

Consider all this in light of what I've been calling *distillation strategies*. We are here taking as the more basic and fundamental knowledge the knowledge embodied in the skills of "tracking down referents" (however that might get done) rather than the knowledge represented in definitions, concepts, propositions, or the like. As is typical in conflicts between distillation strategies, taking one kind of structure or process as more basic than another will have dramatic consequences for how the theory gets spelled out. A highly rationalist preconception about mind as well as a fundamental internalism may be driving us toward a distillation strategy that takes propositions and even definitions as more fundamental and central.

Once again, we see a kind of tension in the choice between distillation strategies for the explanation of some kind of complexity. The suggestion I've been making is the basic, simple, and fundamental knowledge in the knowing meaning resides in skill rather than in the representation of definitions or propositional knowledge. The traditional account has been to take "knowledge that" as basic and find a way to make "knowledge how" an elaboration. The problems we're coming up with might be seen as primarily due to this kind of methodological mistake. By taking skillful knowledge and deictic representation as most basic, we might avoid them.

As in the cases that we've seen throughout the book, we see a kind of shift in the level of description in the taxonomy to be adopted between the task account of an activity and the process account. The task account here is not only a more macro-grain account, but also one that generalizes over properties which don't supervene on just the local structure of the agent. This moral is clear already in chapter 2, where we saw how intentional taxonomy was both more abstract and context-dependent as compared to any locally supervening taxonomy, and in chapter 7, as we saw in the discussion of the context-sensitivity of multiple-cue implementation of skills; and it will again turn up in the next chapter in the discussion of visual perception. The taxonomy for object-oriented generalization about action is embedded, social, and distal, even if that needed to account for the processes producing those systematicities is more local and microstructural.

In the last few chapters, we've seen a transition in thinking about knowledge as needed for action from "knowledge that" to "knowledge how"; that is, from propositional knowledge to skill. We've seen planning and language as showing the central markers of skill: making use of the available information; behavioral success as criterial; implicitness of the knowledge; lack of reportability on the information; often the use of modularized and informationally encapsulated sources of information; and often control placed in the world, in the sense discussed in chapter 6 and brought out by the examples of Simon's ant and Marr's fly.

In the next chapter, I'll turn toward extending these ideas to the case of perception, where perception is seen as an embedded skill. In some ways, this might seem like the most plausible case, but in others, I think it's the least plausible. It's the case of perception, particularly visual perception, in which the metaphor of the veil of perception standing between perceiver and world has been at its most persuasive. But what I'll do now is turn toward the casting off of that veil.

INTERACTIVE
PERCEPTION

I n this chapter, I'll turn to seeing how the theme of more interactive and embedded cognition might also arise for perception—especially *vision*—and how the account might deal with some problems for more traditional accounts of perception. In some ways the case of perception is at first glance the least intuitive. In spite of the fact that perception is, of the activities considered, the most explicitly a process related to the environment—the pickup of information from it—it is also a domain in which the solipsistic intuition has its greatest power. The metaphor of the "veil of perception" is ubiquitous; its underlying theme—that we never really perceptually interact with the world itself, but only our internal representations of it—is at the heart of the internalist conception of mind, the idea of methodological solipsism, and most mainstream accounts of perception. By looking at some facts about the way vision actually seems to work in us, I'll suggest that the current state of the evidence might seem to point us down not only a more embedded and interactive path in the development of a metatheory of perceptual processing, but one also makes important sense of the idea of "direct" perception.

9.1. Perception-as-geometry

The standard account of vision takes it as extracting some kind of a 3-D or even conceptualized representation of the distal array from some kind of 2-D representation of it (roughly, the *proximal stimulus*); as it's put in *The Encyclopedia of Artificial Intelligence*, "The goal of an image understanding system is to transform the two-dimensional data into a description of the three-dimensional spatiotemporal world" [Shapiro 1987, p. 389].

To take perception in this way is to see it as a kind of *inverse optics*. The job of the visual system on this approach is to reconstruct the geometry of the local environment; to implement an inverse of the projection function implemented by the eye that maps distal 3-D surfaces and edges to 2-D regions and curves. The focus is on the reconstruction of the geometric structure of the local environment without regard to its use—on constructing, if you like, a representational "mirror" of the environment.

There is clearly a lot of information lost in the 3-D to 2-D projection that must be recaptured; the 2-D image "does not provide enough information, by itself, to recover the scene. Among others, the depth dimension is collapsed by the projection of a three-dimensional scene to a two-dimensional picture" [Cohen and Feigenbaum 1982, p. 128]. In addition to this geometric collapsing of the scene, "photometrically, the light intensity at each point in an image can result from an infinitude of combinations of illumination, reflectance, and orientation at the corresponding scene point" [Witkin and Tenenbaum 1983, p. 489]. To make up for the loss of information from the projection function, constraints are imposed on the structure of the world in order to insure a unique interpretation of the image. But good candidates for constraints of the interpretation of the 2-D image needed to recover the information lost in the projection from 3-D are hard to come by.

The most central of these involve idealizations about the distal environment, such as rigidity of objects and smooth continuity of surfaces. But as Witkin and Tenenbaum put it in their standard "On the role of structure in vision", "On the whole, the performance and generality of such recovery techniques has been unimpressive . . . [they] have proved fragile and error-prone; while such assumptions may be frequently valid, they also tend to be violated fairly often" [Witkin and Tenenbaum 1983, p. 490]. Marr, for example, clearly makes use of several constraints that will be violated on a regular basis, even in fairly mundane examples of realistic scenes. In fact, some of them are explicitly qualified in this way when offered—e.g., the assumptions that "the loci of discontinuities in depth or in surface orientation are smooth almost everywhere" [Marr 1982, p. 50]. The appropriate idealizations are thus hard to come by; and this only gets worse when trying to find generalizations to play this role that do so within the constraints of a more computationally tractable strategy of using information from local image neighborhoods.[1]

1. Marr considers this problem himself via the classic *aperture* problem; [see Marr 1982, pp. 165–166].

Witkin and Tenenbaum put the point nicely:

> in general, very little information about surface or boundary characteristics can be gleaned from small image neighborhoods that are viewed out of context . . . . occlusion, shadow and reflectance boundaries will often appear locally indistinguishable. Since the information available from a local neighborhood is underdetermined, we know that some form of spatial constraint is therefore required. However, the simple context-independent assumptions (e.g., local continuity) that have been almost universally employed seem both too weak and of limited applicability. [Witkin and Tenenbaum 1983, p. 491]

In short, the reconstruction of the 3-D structure of the environment from a fixed 2-D image of it has turned out to be *hard*. This is of course disconcerting, but it should only motivate a change in the theoretical framework of studying vision if these problems can be significantly lessened by some other available strategy.

One way to make the problem less hard is to reconsider what the job of vision might be. As I've pointed out repeatedly, when we see the function of a process differently, we are forced to attend to different lower-level properties of the device. If the functional account of the device given by the "inverse optics" conception of the task for vision entails lower-level properties that make that task start to seem intractable, we should consider whether a different task account of the process leads us toward more realistic implementational characteristics. Looking for such a different schema for vision brings us to the idea of *animate vision* [Ballard 1991].

9.2. Animate Vision

The central ideas of animate vision might be summarized in terms of three central ways in which it differs from the traditional account: By taking vision to be *task-directed*, by emphasizing the importance of *gaze mechanisms* and the targeting of the fovea, and by facilitating an early and computationally less expensive transition to an *object-centered coordinate system*.

Task-directed Perception. One obvious way to lessen the computational costs of vision is to stop doing everything: Don't try to compute a complete geometric representation of the local distal surroundings, but instead just do what you actually need at any given time. After all, some parts of the local environment may not really change very often (the pattern in my wallpaper is fairly well stabilized at this point, although still pretty complex); and some that change a lot just won't be much worth tracking (the general shifting scene behind you as we stand on the street corner having a conversation). Not devoting resources to these tasks may well save significant power for the hard tasks—like finding some prey hiding in the underbrush, or looking for the spin on Roger Clemens' next pitch. So, to put it crudely, try to get only the things you need.

This can be taken too far; it's part of the point of perception that it informs you about ways that you *didn't* really expect the world to be. So don't throw out monitoring; but don't waste time on things that don't change much, or that do so in ways that largely don't matter to you. In short, compromise on the overall accuracy of representation if you can get more out of what you really want to focus on; let the expense of visual processing be focused and directed at least in part by the task at hand.

These suggestions have a clear compatibility with other kinds of schema for solving problems of intractability in computationally-viewed agents discussed earlier in the book. *Do as little as you can get away with*; don't cross bridges until you get to them. You might not need to cross that bridge anyway, and if you do, the world will often remind you of that when you get there by getting your feet wet. Given the uncertainties of projection in a complex and dynamic environment, first things first; second things may just not make it to the top of the queue anyway.

Gaze and the Fovea. One part of the solution to that question for the human visual system lies in the structure of the eye itself, and the uneven resolution of the eye over various areas of the visual field. The fovea in the human eye covers only about .01% of the visual field area—roughly the size of the thumbnail at arm's length. The fovea is high-resolution area; over the approximately 1° of visual angle it covers, the resolution is better than that in the periphery by an order of magnitude [Ballard 1991]. This allows for high acuity at the focus point without giving up the virtues of a large field of view. Making the most of such a variable-resolution sensor requires being able to accurately and quickly adjust the targeting of the high-resolution fovea, both for tracking moving objects and scanning various parts of scenes. That is, you should have fast and accurate gaze control mechanisms to compliment foveal vision.

The human visual system does it in just this way. A variable-resolution detector is combined with very fast mechanisms for tracking and scanning. Quick scanning of a scene by *saccadic eye movements* every 300 ms or so is routine. Further, the pattern of scanning is highly sensitive to the task at hand—e.g., questions about the ages of people in a picture will elicit saccades bringing the fovea largely to the faces [Yarbus 1967].

Reducing the complexity of the task by using gaze fixation mechanisms first is no gain if those mechanisms themselves reintroduce the same sorts of complexity. But the outlook from the current vantage point would seem to be that they don't. There are some striking results around. Olson and Coombs [1990] give some impressive results for visual tracking using low-level processes of stereopsis. And Horswill and Brooks [1988] showed striking success in tracking and following slowish medium-sized objects (e.g., a radio-controlled toy truck) using simple blob-matching at a resolution of 32×28 and a sample rate of 5 per second. The fact seems to be that moderately low-level hacks can facilitate fairly successful tracking by using simple, fast, tight feedback-loop controlled tracking mechanisms to provide gaze fixation.

So we reduce complexity by using a highly targetable sensor where much of the work of targeting might be done by moderately simple low-level feedback loops from sensor output to gaze control. But in the process, we can realize further advantages. In particular, this general strategy for visual sensing can facilitate a turn toward using object-centered coordinate frames at a very early point in the process of vision—perhaps the most significant advantage of animate vision systems.

Object-centered Coordinates. The early shift to object-centered representation certainly contrasts with an account like Marr's, where the turn occurs quite late in the process—roughly at the point where categorical parsing or recognition takes place. There is a seeming advantage of this. Many of the early calculations can be done in a framework of image-oriented computation. For Marr, it is only at this final step in the process of vision that we must "abandon the luxury of a viewer-centered coordinate frame on which all representations discussed hitherto have been based because of their intimate connection with the imaging process" [Marr 1982, p. 295]. Finally, at the point of object recognition, we must go to a representation where "the pieces and articulation of a shape need to be described not relative to the viewer but relative to a frame of reference based on the shape itself" [Marr 1982, p. 296].

But there is an obvious computational drawback to this approach. If the processing gets done in the image overall, then computational resources are expended on parts of the image that may be insignificant for current purposes. The motivation for trying to find *local* strategies for image interpretation is clear; it's just [see Witkin and Tenenbaum 1983, above] that the information in the image doesn't seem to support them. The task-directedness of the allocation of computational resources is, to some extent, violated by this approach. But by starting with an object-centered coordinate frame at an earlier point in processing, we reduce this complexity in several ways. For example, complex computations to determine the relative motions of object and backdrop that might have required iteration of the image as a whole might now be done in more local image space. [See Ballard 1990.] And relative depth computations that make use of the shifts in parallax in front of and behind the fixation frame for gaze are decidedly less expensive than subject-centered means of accomplishing these tasks. [See Ballard and Ozcandarli 1988.]

If we make the shift to taking seriously the "animate vision paradigm," what do we get? The process of vision in many ways becomes more one of interactivity with and embedding in the environment; a process highly dependent for the character of its computational tasks on a very particular kind of embodiment, and on its interrelationships with particular complex abilities built into the device's data collection mechanisms. It cuts its computational burdens by using this interactivity to facilitate quick and early representation in the coordinate system eventually necessary for use—the one that represents the objects, to put it a little philosophically, as they are in the world rather than as they are as "raw appearance."

Object-centered systems also have the advantage of being natural candidates for representational systems that rely heavily on indexical reference. An object is presented as the current object of fixation (*that* object) while particular descriptive accounts of that object may be grossly underdeveloped, and in no way rich enough to discriminate it from other objects—as when we track a particular point of light moving among an indeterminate swarm of such points. The particularity of that point is given by the tracking that the visual system does.[2] In such cases, the work of linking up with the object in the world that is the referent for the organism's state is (as in the cases considered in chapter 8) not done within the organism's conceptual space, but rather by the structure of the agent's embodiment—in this case, the interactive relationship between targetable sensors and the local environment.

In part, we are taking advantage of the same general strategy discussed in the preceeding chapters of letting the world "be its own best model"—i.e., of storing information in the world rather than in our heads whenever it's feasible. In the case of vision, we avoid having to build and maintain a complete, high-resolution visual model of the environment by scanning for what we need, and letting the constancy of the layout provide the underpinnings of the phenomenological constancy of perception.

9.3. "Direct" Perception?

The idea of "direct" perception is most closely associated with the work of J. J. Gibson [1986], although threads of such a view can be found throughout the history of philosophical considerations of perception. In recent times, the general perspective has taken on a kind of behaviorist tone, which has been encouraged by some of Gibson's own discussion of the idea. What I'd like to do in this section is to recast an account of "direct" perception in such a way as to remove both the behaviorist and the anti-information-processing themes of Gibson's account. There is, in my view, a substantial germ of truth in the perspective of "direct perception" that I'd like to hold onto; at least part of my task right now will be to bring that out.

Marr pays slight homage to Gibson and his approach, emphasizing the value of both a bottom-up perspective on processing and emphasizing the richness of the information available in the light— both clearly Gibsonian themes. However, he balks at the suggestion that vision should not be seen as an information-processing task, but instead as a task of pure transduction—of tuning transducers to (what Gibson calls) the "affordances" in the environment. As Marr sees it, Gibson's mistake "results from a failure to realize two things. First, the detection of physical invariants, like image surfaces, is exactly and precisely an information-processing prob-

2. Just like Kant said: Particularity in space and time are given in the synthesis of the manifold of intuition.

lem . . . second, he vastly underrated the sheer difficulty of such detection" [Marr 1982, p. 30].

I share the concern about Gibson's denial that perception should be seen as an information-processing task, as well as those voiced by Fodor and Pylyshyn [1981] about the extent to which Gibson's variant of the "direct" perception view ignores the importance of seeing mental states as exhibiting *intentionality*. But these suppositions seem to me inessential to a reasonable account of the directness of perception. So rather than defending Gibson against his critics, I'll just try to make sense out of the idea that some notion of "direct" perception might be both coherent and even possibly *true*.

It's not at all unnatural to take the idea of "direct" perception as being at first glance nearly absurd. The idea that what we really directly perceive is *distal* objects in the environment rather than some inner representation of them (like, say, the retinal image) might seem to require some kind of "occult" causation at a distance, violate the idea that perception is in some way or other a physical process in the world, and that it is in some way mediated by light. But I think the view is far from incoherent. Rather, I think it can be seen as a moderately straightforward claim about the appropriate methodological and metatheoretical point of view to take in the analysis of perception in an environment. In large part, making that clear will be the focus of what follows.

But there is a more general kind of strategy that underlies this kind of opposition to "direct" perception which I would also like to comment on. I'll use the discussion of direct perception as a kind of case study in bringing this out. There is a widespread tendency to argue against a methodological outlook by either explicitly or implicitly appealing to its *incoherence* or to an inability to see how it could *possibly* be true (even if it might be *in fact* false).

So in trying to show how the direct perception story might possibly be right, what I explicitly won't make is any kind of "ordinary language" philosophy argument. Shaw and Bransford [1977], for example, try to argue that direct perception is coherent from a kind of Rylean ground—by showing that the contrast case violates some constraints on ordinary language use. In this way, you take up the challenge of incoherence and try to turn the tables on it. Rather than trying to show that it's the contrast case of "indirect" that *really* violates the principles of ordinary language use, I'll instead try to transcend the "your view's more incoherent than mine" game.

By making such methodological arguments into arguments of a kind of conceptual analysis, we miss important possibilities. A more forceful argument against a methodological outlook should "cut it enough slack" to make it clear how it *could* be correct, and then show how it fails to meet reasonable empirical requirements. To do otherwise is to take aim at a straw man. There is an important and legitimate difference in methodology between viewing perception as "direct" and as "indirect" or "representational." To reduce the question to a kind of verbal dispute or conceptual triviality strips us of the possibility of getting a solution to a real substantive claim. As I pointed out in chapter 3, similar situations arise in other cases across the science which turn on finding a most appropriate level or levels of explanation of some behavioral systematicity of a complex system.

9.4. Combatting Illusion

The intuitive argument against direct perception is a simple one: the argument from illusion—or if you like, the "dominance of the proximal." You can have the percept without the object as long as you have the right proximal stimulus; but you can't have the percept without the right proximal stimulus, even if you do have the right object there. That is, set the proximal stimulus up right, and whether or not the distal stimulus is there is irrelevant to perception.

There are two sides to rebutting the "dominance of the proximal" line: On the one hand, we need to see how variance in the proximal stimulus is (within interesting bounds) irrelevant to the percept. That is, we need to see how a fixed *distal* layout and a varying *proximal* stimuli might commonly underlie a *fixed* character to visual perception. To do this is to bring out the way in which *the mapping from proximal stimuli to visual percepts is many-to-one*—i.e., how percepts are *multiply realizable* with respect to proximal stimuli. And on the other hand, we need to see how variance in the *distal* layout—even given a fixed proximal stimulus—can affect the percept; that is, how a fixed *proximal* stimuli but a different *distal* layout might commonly underlie different visual perceptions. And this is to bring out how *the mapping from visual percepts to proximal stimuli is many-to-one*—i.e., how percepts are *context-dependent* with respect to proximal stimuli.

What's critical for my point is to show how context-dependence (and multiple realizability, as discussed in chap. 3) can bring out a clear sense in which the connection between percept and distal layout is more intimate than that between percept and proximal stimulus. What reason is there to see the percept as being produced *by virtue of* the properties of the layout rather than the proximal stimulus? How, contrary to the standard argument from illusion, might the properties of the distal layout mask variations in the proximal stimulus from the perceptual content, rather than vice-versa?

Proximal-stimulus-to-percept as many-to-one. How is the visual percept multiply realizable with respect to the proximal stimulus? First of all, note that the level of grain of the conscious percept would seem to be significantly more abstract than that of the proximal stimulus; in fact, it seems roughly at the level of abstraction of a categorization of the distal display: The chair across the room looks stationary to me, and I will treat it that way in my actions dealing with it, in spite of the fact that from the point of view of retinal display (or even the light that gets to my body) it is jumping around (via my movements—both saccadic and gross bodily), in various resolutions (as it comes in and out of the focus of my fovea), and so on. To put it more suggestively: If you could view a movie where the frames are simply a representation of the retinal image (or other retinally indexed display) of someone else's visual system, what you would see would be a blurry (except in the very center) image that jumped around like a videotape shot by a hyperkinetic 3-year-old.

The character of the phenomenology of perception is, to put it simply, a more natural match onto the character of the distal layout than onto the transduced pattern of light. The mapping from streams of proximal stimuli to perceptual states is many-to-one. Lots of different proximal stimuli and scanning patterns will provide the same percept. In vision, what's constant over a span of, say, 250 ms or more, is not any kind of proximal stimuli. Even with a stationary organism and scene, the display of ambient light on the retina is shifting chaotically along with the saccadic eye movements.[3]

3. It may be even worse: Even with a fixed visual array, different searches can shift the focus of processing from one place to another in the visual input. This decoupling of visual *attention* lets us have the same proximal stimulus, same transducer outputs, *and the same eye-control events* in two different cases; but if the focus of visual attention varies across the two cases, we'd have a different percept. [See Tsal 1983.]

So you *can* fix the distal stimulus (under at least some kinds of normal perceptual conditions) and vary the proximal stimuli (within certain bounds) while leaving the variations in proximal stimuli irrelevant. As long as the stream of proximal stimuli is fixed in the right (roughly, normal) way, which precise pattern of scanning you engage in is irrelevant. The variations due to the different possible patterns of scanning are, if you like, masked from the percept. Within the bounds of *normal functioning of the perceptual apparatus*, a fixed distal layout will support constancy in perception across some notable variations in the proximal stimulus. Turning off all the lights won't count as normal operation (for vision), but normal scanning and moving will.

Proximal-stimulus-to-percept as one-to-many. But if you fix the *proximal* stimulus—e.g., the ambient light array hitting the retina—and vary the properties of the *distal* layout, then under normal conditions you will *not* necessarily have prevented the percept from varying as a result of the distal changes. Visual perception *can* be affected by manipulations of the layout that don't affect the light *if the organism knows about those changes in the layout*—that is, if those changes in the layout can in some way affect the interactive process between organism and environment. The paths by which changes in the distal layout can have an effect on perception aren't in any way occult; they're just various other routes by which changes in the distal layout come to causally affect the organism in *some* way or other.

Nobody is claiming that changes in the distal layout can affect changes in perception without *any* mechanisms allowing them to causally affect the organism at *all*. You certainly need *some* mechanism by which the relevant features of the distal layout affect the overall state of the organism. And there are various straightforward routes by which experience of objects in the world can affect how we perceptually process the information we detect. For example, other sensory modalities can certainly prime vision to interpret and search the environment in a different way than it would have otherwise. Trivial cases would include such things as getting audible instructions for interpreting an ambiguous or degraded picture: Telling the subject what the object is can bring on recognition, as evidenced both by the subjective gestalt shift and by the facilitation of the extraction of further information from the

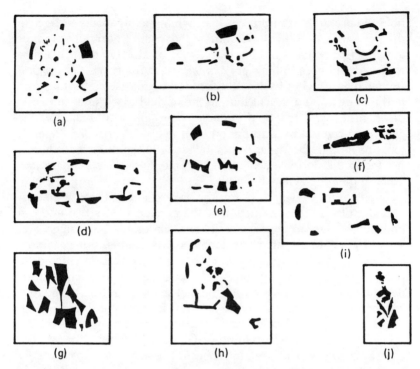

Figure 9.1. Ambiguous pictures: (a) clock; (b) airplane; (c) typewriter; (d) bus; (e) elephant; (f) saw, (g) shoe, (h) boy with dog, (i) roadster, and (j) violin. (From Leeper 1935.)

picture (e.g., the orientation of the object) [see Fig. 9.1; also McClamrock 1989].[4]

Here, by changing the distal stimulus *and* the effects on the organism through other sense modalities, we change the way the very same local proximal stimulus for vision is interpreted; and this changed the perceptual content. This is an example of a constant proximal stimulus but with different patterns of activity for the organism. In this case, the different pattern of activity is essentially internal; it's just different *processing* of the stimulus on the basis of other information in the system. But the different pattern of activity may well be activity in the external environment as well. To

---

4. The *McGurk effect* [McGurk and MacDonald 1976]—which illustrates the effects of visual presentation of the speaker's face on the perception of phonemes—is a nice example of this phenomenon in speech perception.

hold the proximal stimulus constant while the organism engages in different activity in the environment that would normally produce a *changed* proximal stimulus is likely to produce nausea. If I turn my head and eyes to the right *and the visual field comes along with it* (rather than flowing back to the left as I turn), the perceptual content will be quite different than in the normal case—and in a quite disorienting way. It would be a more pronounced version of the effect you can get by pushing on your eyeball with your finger: It looks as though the *layout* is moving along with your eye (or head), not (as in the normal case) as though the layout is stationary and you are panning across it.[5]

Even within a given modality, the context-dependence of the current stimulus in the production of the percept allows that you can both know the strategies, beliefs, and biases of the system, and know the character of the instantaneous stimulus, but *not* know the percept, because its position in the ongoing and interactive process might still be critical. An obvious example of such context-dependence simply falls out of the fact that perception is taken as a transformation from 2-D to 3-D. Even in a simple line drawing, the role of a given line depends on the surrounding context: The orientation of a line which on the 2-D image is slanted like this "/" can contribute any of a wide range of possible 3-D projections to the percept—e.g., the orientation of the edge of a tall building as we look up at it, or the slanted line of one leg of a tripod.

A similar point holds for contexts extended in time rather than in space: The very same proximal stimulus might be a part of seeing something as a square surface with a particular orientation when it occurs in one sequence, but a part of seeing something as a trapezoidal surface with a different orientation when you see it in a different sequence. The underdetermination here that occurs in cases of moving images is, of course, the standard "structure from motion" problem. Ullman's rotating cylinders [Fig. 9.2] illustrate the problem nicely. At any given instant, the dots on the two rotating cylinders present a roughly random display of dots; but viewing the structure in motion leaves the three-dimensional structure of

5. It's in part this kind of detailed interactive basis of perception that makes brain-in-a-vat stories—everybody's favorite 20th-century version of Descartes' evil genius—so wild. A convincing illusion would require an unbelievably complex and delicate balance of interactions between motor-control signals from the brain and the sensory input signals. Better to just build a world and get those things for free—like God did.

the cylinders clearly visible. The underlying shapes that form the perceptual gestalt are underdetermined by the moment, but filled out by the temporal context surrounding any given moment.

The idea of perceptual gestalts extended in time is perhaps the most common kind of example of a gestalt as a unity as opposed to a series of discrete parts. The unity of a melody, to use perhaps the most ubiquitous example, needn't at all lie in representing it as a piece in conscious experience at any moment. It's instead an ongoing activity; the experience of the melody might even seem essentially extended in time, and its unity in the flow of the process.

As we move away from the phenomenology of immediate perception to reconsider the unity in more conceptual level judgement and belief, this way of seeing the unity of perceptual gestalts naturally suggests a way of thinking about the dependence of the unity of conceptual judgement and belief on the embedding context.

A further way in which embedding context determines the content of perception beyond the underdetermining local proximal stimulus is by past inputs (to either this modality or others) which change the system's internal structure—that is, by some kind of learning or training. This obviously effects the way in which different *types* of stimuli are perceived: The perceptual system can be altered by evolution or training so that differences in the world the organism has confronted or has been built for can make a difference in perceptual state without that difference showing up in the local proximal stimulus. Clear examples here are to be found in speech perception; e.g., where we draw the line between phonemes (and thus words) depends importantly on the stimuli we get from the speech produced in our local language community [see Miller 1982]. Other such cases of perceptual training are easy to find; e.g., exactly the same acoustic signal used to sound like a simple note on a piano, but now has a distinctive waver of the beat frequency produced by the frequency difference between the piano's strings.

These cases are, however, clearly of a somewhat different sort than those noted above. The features of external context which are determining the percept beyond what the proximal stimulus gives are ones that have now been compiled into the organism (see chap. 7). Because of this, it wouldn't be unnatural to think that the current state of the organism, given it's *currently* relatively fixed strategies for interpreting the environment—*screens off* these past contextual features from the effects they now have on current perceptions. This isn't, however, quite right; and I think these cases are

A

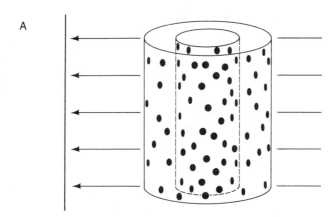

Figure 9.2. Ullman's rotating cylinders. (a) Dots from the two cylinders are projected onto a flat screen as indicated by the arrows, producing a series of apparently random-dot frames (b). When seen as a movie, the rotating cylinders are clearly visible. (From Marr 1982.)

closer to the perceptual gestalt cases given above than they might seem at first glance. But that's a problem that I'll leave until the discussion of *intentional causation* in chapter 10.

So on the one hand, fixing the proximal stimuli or the transducer outputs doesn't mask variation in the layout from variation in visual perception because of the context-dependence and interactivity of vision: How you look, scan, and move on the basis of the distal layout makes a difference. And on the other, fixing the *layout* and allowing a range of variation in the proximal stimuli may provide a fixed perceptual content as long as those proximal stimuli are kept within the bounds of the normal perception of that scene, since the mapping of sequences of proximal stimuli to perceptual contents is many-to-one. So it looks like the argument from illusion just doesn't carry the load.

What's critical for my point is to show how context-dependence and multiple realizability can bring out a clear sense in which the connection between percept and distal layout is more intimate than that between percept and proximal stimulus. What reason is there to see the percept as being produced *by virtue of* the properties of the layout rather than the proximal stimulus? How, contrary to the standard argument from illusion, might the properties of the distal layout mask variations in the proximal stimulus from the perceptual content, rather than vice-versa?

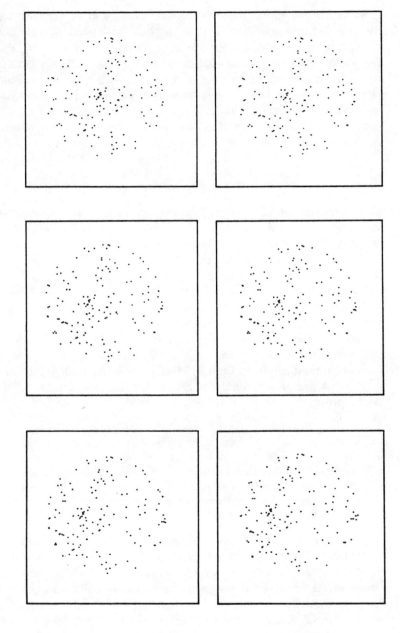

What's right about direct perception is *not* that perception isn't information-processing, or that perception isn't hard, or that perception isn't mediated by light or by internal mechanisms. It's that the systematicity of perceptual content is roughly the systematicity of the distal layout and *not* of the proximal stimuli. Perceptual states are produced *in virtue of* properties of the distal layout. Just as properties of groups rather than individuals can be implicated in evolutionary effects, properties of environments rather than stimuli can be implicated in perceptual ones.

9.5. Distillation Again

The deeper problem with the illusion argument and the idea that the proximal stimulus must mask the distal layout from perceptual content is that it assumes a certain kind of strategy of *distillation* in the explanation of visual perception. By taking the fundamental and essential idea of visual perception to be that of taking a 2-D retinal image with the subject's frame of reference and inferring a 3-D layout from it (and no other aspect of our contact with the world), we miss something critical about vision: Vision is *activity*; not just internal information-processing, but the active and animate probing of the environment.

As I pointed out in chapter 7, Marr pays explicit allegiance to a methodological position that led him down the now-standard path. As he put it,

> If, using the human visual processor, we can experimentally isolate a process and show that it can still work well [e.g., by "providing images in which . . . all kinds of information except one have been removed and then to see whether we can make use of just that one kind"], then it cannot require complex interaction with other parts of vision and can therefore be understood relatively well on its own. [1982, p. 101]

A central part of Marr's worry here is about the use of top-down information flow in visual processing. As he says, the idea that vision is largely driven top-down by general knowledge and expectations is "completely wrong . . . even in difficult circumstances shapes could be determined by vision alone" [ibid., p. 36]. But surely normal vision is in some key ways driven by more general cognitive features—not just the kind discussed in chapter 7 which might provide top-down input to the processing that takes place between retina and 3-D model, but even more fundamentally, ones that affect how the resources of vision get allocated to the scene we're presented with, as the task-dependent patterns of saccadic eye movement show.

In fact, the kinds of features that a more embedded and animate visual system exhibit are not necessarily incompatible with what strike me as the more basic underlying motivations for the above "decomposition" distillation strategy discussed earlier. Perhaps the most central aspect of animate vision is the use of gaze fixation mechanisms to transform the computational problem of 3-D vision at a very early point. But rapid and short feedback loops to controllers for gaze fixation are clearly entirely compatible with modularity, and it's clearly the central link in the immediate move to an object-centered coordinate frame. And even the task-directed nature of scanning behavior needn't impugn a high degree of visual modularity. The targeting of the transducers is sensitive to the explicit beliefs and projects of the organism; but that's entirely compatible with as much modularity as you like between transduction and 3-D representation.

Part of the problem in finding the right distillation strategy is that the human visual system is awfully good under highly impoverished conditions of various kinds. On the one hand, extremely rapid images flashed by are processed fairly effectively: People are quite good at tachistoscopic presentation of images where no scanning is possible because of the short time duration, no motion is available to give cues for depth in relative motion, and so on. On the other hand, we are also extremely good with impoverished information of other kinds—for example, the form-from-motion cases discussed above.

This embarrassment of riches is problematic because of its tendency to encourage different kinds of distillation strategies. One is the inverse optics strategy. Our ability to get an enormous amount of information from a full image presented very quickly and without motion and without ability to scan supports this kind of distillation. The form-from-motion successes indicate a quite different strategy where the animate and 3-D character of the scene and the agent's relationship to it are critical parts of what makes the perceptual task doable.

The moral that I've been encouraging here need not be taken as suggesting that static 2-D vision doesn't do a reasonable task when it's required to. Rather, the suggestion has been that the task of vision is a particular kind of task—one of providing for problem-solving and planning a kind of representation of the environment that is going to be useful for those processes. This task conception for vision takes it as abstracting away from particular presentations of objects in the local environment to a characterization of the type and relative location of those objects. To put it in a very crude way, my beliefs and goals with respect to the objects in my environment don't shift as my perspective on them shifts. The systematicity of action with respect to the environment is (within the bounds of normal perceptual presentation) indifferent to the exact nature of that presentation, the angle at which it's seen, and so on. It's the indifference of this kind of systematicity to the varieties of implementation for it that has been all along the marker of the appropriate level of abstraction about the task.

A thorough rejection of individualism in even perceptual psychology involves seeing the perceptual processes as not solipsistic ones defined over transducer outputs, but as processes whose unity requires animate vision, moving around and scanning in a particular kind of world. This distal-object orientation is what makes the current view of perception of a piece with the general account I've been giving all along, and will also be a key theme in the philosophical question that follows.

PART FOUR

Philosophical Implications

CHAPTER
T E N

INTENTIONALITY
AND ITS OBJECTS

S everal distinct threads have now been brought together here that suggest the general worth of the "embedded" perspective. The new "causal" theory of reference discussed in chapter 8 focuses on causal history and processes outside the individual subject as critical to the determination of meaning. The account of embedded cognition and perception in chapters 7 and 9 have illustrated some of the increasing emphasis and expanding successes of information-processing accounts of complex behavior that give a central position to the ecological analysis of the organism and its exploitation of external regularities.

All the accounts share a kind of denial of logical elegance in favor of the exploitation of general contingencies, and an adherence to a general approach that emphasizes the exploitation of multiple sources of information through various strategies rather than taking some one process or strategy as central and essential to our skills and dispositions. The idea that there must be one fundamental process to account for the basic solving of the task—rather than the task solution being a more emergent property of a variety of processes in the organism which fit together under the normal conditions of application—is in some ways the fundamental individualistic/solipsistic bias; and the detailed rejection of that in favor of an approach emphasizing robustness and redundancy or multiple and varied informational routes to and from the environment has been the central theme of the book so far.

In this final section of the book, I'll turn to some more traditionally "philosophical" questions and look at how the perspective I've been offering might deal with them. One reason for doing so is my belief that these topics often provide basic (and sometimes hidden) motivations for metatheoretical views. But I also think that an important part of evaluating an outlook is to see what more general consequences might follow from it. Real theory evaluation is hardly monotonic—or as the saying goes, "One philosopher's *modus ponens* is another's *modus tollens.*"

First, I'll look at how the embedded outlook can give a better account of the "object-oriented" nature of intentionality, and by doing so, help resolve some of the puzzles about intentionality—including the possibility of intentional causation, the intentionality of sensation, and the "symbol-grounding" problem. Then in chapter 11, I'll discuss the even murkier issue of *subjectivity*, and how the current discussion might suggest a perspective which is neither *reductionist* (or *eliminativist*) nor *anti-materialist*, but which provides for a kind of *autonomy* of the phenomenological. And then in the final chapter, I'll explore some of the connections between the current account and a kind of naturalistic version of the general perspective of *existential* phenomenology. I'll focus there on the potential relevance of three "phenomenological" ideas: the distinction between *real* and *intentional* aspects of conscious acts (Husserl's distinction between *noesis* and *noema*); the notion of phenomenological *bracketing* as methodological approach to the mind; and the idea of *existential* phenomenology and its focus on the dependence of the nature of consciousness on the nature of the world.

But first, intentionality. The general conception of intentionality that emerges within the view of mind as essentially embedded is clearly one that emphasizes "directedness on an object" over what Brentano called "intentional in-existence"; What consequences should that shift in emphasis have?

Recall that in chapter 3, I tried to fill in a sense in which distal causes might be seen as in an important sense more immediate than more proximal ones—an immediacy based on sameness of level of organization rather than spatial-temporal proximity. This possibility was realized in cases where there were multiple paths between objects and behaviors or internal states which shared systematically only their object-directed properties. Salient behavioral patterns may be mediated by different mechanisms in different cases—even with the same organism. This idea of multiple routes between behaviors and the objects systematically linked to them (as discussed in chap. 3) fits naturally with the idea of exploiting a rich and redundant set of cues provided by the complex environment. If the cuing for the presence of objects, satisfaction of goals, and so on is done through various routes depending on contacts, then we should naturally expect to see systematicity of behavior with respect to the object or goal and not any one of the particular routes.

This fundamental object-directedness is an obvious candidate for the consideration of the object-directedness of *intentionality*. In what follows, I'll consider some of the contemporary worries about intentionality in the light of this.

10.1. Varieties of Semantic Impotence

One of the standard and widespread worries from cognitivists concerns the causal power of *semantic* properties of states of organisms. On the one hand, cognitivists who take intentional explanation and generalization seriously want the contents of our intentional states to in some sense govern our behavior; on the other, they worry deeply about "occult" causation. Surely this was one of the underlying themes in chapter 2. As Zenon Pylyshyn puts the worry, "The semantics of representations cannot literally cause a system to behave the way it does; only the material form of the representation is causally efficacious . . . What actually do the causing are certain physical properties of the representational state—but in a way that reflects the representational state's content" [Pylyshyn 1984, p. 39]. This worry makes for deep slurs against the efficacy of meaning; it motivates Dennett [1990] to see it as "impotent," and Schiffer [1987] to disparage it as "an excrescence" that "does nothing and explains nothing." Colorful slurs aside, this concern is clearly widely thought to lead to some kind of epiphenomenalism about content. But the seeds of an account of what's wrong with this were given in chapters 2 and 3; I'll now turn to filling those out.

In light of the discussion in chapters 1 and 3, we can quickly dispense with one form of the claim of epiphenomenalism about meanings. If semantic properties of representational systems supervene on some properties at a lower level of organization, that alone in no way entails that the higher-level properties are causally impotent. As I pointed out in part 1: Higher-level properties can be causally potent, and can even be the preferred level of explanation for a given phenomenon.

There's another fairly standard way to point out that various kinds of properties are epiphenomenal—particularly distinctively mental properties, like the semantic and phenomenological ones—that I should sidestep right from the start. This involves appealing to the intuition that something could have the same information-processing (or perhaps even physical) structure that I do without having the same mental (e.g., intentional, phenomenological, whatever) properties that I do. This line is perhaps most common when discussing the possibility of "absent qualia" zombies, although this kind of argument about intentionality has become more widespread following Searle's [1980] introduction of such arguments into the anti-AI debate.

I'm personally less than overwhelmed by the intuition of this possibility; but for present purposes, it's enough to point out that even accepting the possibility of an "absent Q" zombie should not commit one to the view that Q properties are epiphenomenal. As Ned Block has pointed out [Block 1980, pp. 262–263], such an inference to the epiphenomenal status of features conflates two distinct understandings of an "absent Q" intuition. Taken in the weak sense—as claiming that a state in some information-processing system could have the causal role of one of my conscious states without the normal Q properties—the hypothesis may be true, but doesn't entail the appropriate epiphenomenalism. Showing that something else might play a given functional role while lacking some particular property doesn't show that property to be epiphenomenal; hydraulic fluid in a brake system is not epiphenomenal, although the same functional role might be performed by cables or rods. But taken in the strong sense—as claiming that *my* cognitive states could lack their Q properties but have the same causal roles—the intuition is far from obvious. There is no reason (independent of the general disposition to epiphenomenalism here) to assume the strong form of the intuition; but it's the *stronger* reading that's needed to claim that phenomenological properties are epiphenomenal.

But clearly there is a deeper worry about the efficacy of the intentional than these, and Fred Dretske [1990] characterizes it nicely. As he puts it:

> if meaning supervenes, at least in part, on the extrinsic properties of an event—historical and relational facts that need not be mirrored in the event's current . . . physical constitution or structure—then, if A causes B, the fact, if it is a fact, that A means M will not—indeed, cannot—figure in a causal explanation of B. It cannot because, in similar circumstances, an event lacking this meaning, but otherwise the same, will have exactly the same effects. [p. 9]

> . . . the historical and relational differences . . . are *screened off* from the explanation of the object's behavior. [p. 8]

The central idea is twofold: First, the intentional properties of representations, being determined in part by the representations' historical and contextual properties, are more distal from—and thus is some way *screened off* from—the effects the representational state has on behavior than are its syntactic properties. What role they have is only via the syntax of the representation; e.g., by causing particular representations to be tokened at particular times, or by contributing to setting the system up—through evolution or training—so that the representations correlate with the environment in a particular way.[1] And second, this screening off of the intentional properties from behavioral effects by the syntactic ones is such that it leaves those intentional properties explanatorily irrelevant.

10.2. Revitalizing the Intentional

Both parts of the above suggestion are problematic. The discussion in chapter 2 should have made clear what's wrong with the first part: The contextual relationships of representations on which their meanings depend are *not* necessarily more distant from the representation's effect on behavior than their syntactic properties are. The causal properties of representations don't supervene only on local syntax. In fact, the causal properties of representations depend on external semantic properties—not just to set them up, but to implement them in current thought and action. As I pointed out in chapter 2 (and several times since, especially in chap. 7), social and environmental mechanisms of all sorts may well mediate the difference in causal powers of mental states. The intentional properties depend on mechanisms that are larger than the syntax of the representation and extend in the world—including the reactive properties of the organism, and the social properties that help fix meaning and behavior. Semantic properties of representational states aren't screened off because the interactivity and context-dependence at the intentional level of organization makes those external features a critical part of the current mechanisms of causation of the intentionally systematic behavior.

1. The idea that intentional (and teleological) explanation involves appeal to *future* objects or *goals* is also an obvious part of what makes them distinctive. The puzzle here as to how this works is surely to be resolved by some kind of *feedback loop* [see Elster 1983] from the type of object in the past. See McClamrock [1993] for a consideration of this strategy in functional explanation generally.

The second part of the worry about intentional impotence—that intentional properties are screened off from behavioral effects by the syntactic properties in such a way as to make those intentional properties explanatorily irrelevant—is also problematic. After all, to some extent the causal properties of representation will show up in their syntax. To the extent that they do, should we see the meaning of representation as impotent?

Non-local historical and relational differences relevant to a representation's meaning are seen as screened off from the explanation of the organism's behavior because more proximal causes screen off more distal ones. But certainly the fact that there are more proximal causes of some specified effect doesn't mean that the more distal ones should be seen as impotent or irrelevant.

This is true in two senses—one of which is fairly trivial: Just because one cause is more distal than another doesn't mean that it's explanatorily *irrelevant*. Smoking cigarettes can be a critical cause and piece of the explanation for lung cancer, in spite of the fact that there are no doubt more proximal physiological causes of the cancer. Similarly, the lack of gas in the tank is critical in the causal account of the car's failure to run, even though the lack of hot, expanding gases in the combustion chambers of the engine at the appropriate time is obviously a more proximal cause. More distal causes aren't impotent or irrelevant. Similarly for the mental cases: If some syntactic (or neural) properties of the system are more proximal to some behavioral effect, that doesn't mean that the more distal causes—inside or outside the organism—are causally impotent or explanatorily irrelevant. The fact that there's ice cream in front of me is a critical link in my coming to eat the ice cream.

10.3. Distal and Intentional Causes

There is also an even stronger sense of the potency of distal causation which I want to advocate—the sense I spelled out at the end of chapter 3. More distal properties can have a kind of explanatory priority over more proximal ones that can be brought out by using the notion of *screening off* in conjunction with those of multiple realizability and context-dependence. I think that in the end the critical problem for intentionality and causation is whether distal properties can override proximal ones; the story given in chapter 3 brings out a way in which this is in fact possible.

The key idea for the alternative proposed here is that object-oriented accounts of behavior are necessitated by multiple paths to the object in behavior. Multiple criteria are the mark of behavior that exhibits object-directed or goal-directed behavior. In fact, even mainstream cognitivists like Pylyshyn [1984] sell this point hard to motivate the importance of a content level of explanation of behavioral systematicities:

> the behavior of the system cannot be explained in terms of a chain of causal laws connecting such extrinsic entities as those mentioned in accounts (4) and (5) to the current state of the system. The reason for this has already been discussed in chapter 1, that is, the causal chain would have to contain an arbitrarily large disjunction of possible physical causes, since the relevant connections between the extrinsic events and the current state includes such relations as: being told about them by someone, reading about them, inferring from what one has seen or heard, and so on. Neither numbers nor the anticipation of help can in any sense be viewed as causal inputs to the system. [P. 25]

At the end of chapter 3, I characterized the possibility of a more distal cause of an event being preferred over a more proximal one in explanation. For this to be the case, the more distal cause should be at the right level of organization to specify properties in virtue of which the event occurs. In cases where there is no class of more proximal properties in virtue of which a particular class of effects takes place (even if each *case* in that class has some more proximal cause at a lower level of organization), the distal cause may screen off the more proximal ones; the effect correlates with the distal cause regardless (more or less) of the precise route by which that distal cause has its proximal effects. In such "multiple path" cases (characterized in chap. 3), there is no intermediate more proximal stage in the explanation that screens off the intentional properties, because of widespread multiple realizability and context-dependence at the intermediate and proximal stage. Whether more proximal causes screen off more distal ones is dependent on the kind of phenomena to be explained.

Syntactic properties don't screen off intentional ones when you pick the right generalizations to be explained.[2] It might turn out that the intentional properties are the more relevant ones for

2. This is not entirely incompatible with Dretske's own line on intentional causation: On his account, "the meaning of neural events is . . . epiphenomenal if all we

explanation, because they actually screen off the intermediate syntactic ones from the behavioral generalizations. Intentional systematicities screen off the particulars of implementation. Thus the *types* of behavior are *better* linked with semantic properties.

The description under which objects in the world exhibit systematic links with your behavior is roughly the distal object-oriented one. It's the robust distalcause that has a systematic causal relationship to behavior, and the routes by which that distal cause affects you (by hearing about it, seeing it, whatever) don't matter so much. A wide variety of proximal forms for information are compatible with/converging on the same distal state/property, and it's the distal state and its grain of taxonomy with respect to which behavior is systematic.

This systematicity of behavior at the level of object is a central motivation for the cognitivists for conjecturing a level of internal representational systematicity that corresponds to it. Although this is one possible way to achieve that systematicity, it's obviously not the only one. Furthermore, there may well be many ways in which allowing the systematicity to emerge from something other than systematic representations at the appropriate level allows for a more plausible mechanism in computational terms of tractability of task, as well as in terms of the possibility of such a mechanism evolving and learning its skills. The mark of an appropriate domain for intentional explanation is when distal states of the world screen off more proximal ones with respect to the behavioral systematicities of the device or organism; the mechanisms by which that happens are open.

So there's no reason at all why the causal potency of the semantic has to commit you to anything objectionable. Dennett is wrong in saying that "a semantic engine . . . is a mechanistic impossibility—like a perpetual motion machine, but a useful idealization in setting the specs for actual mechanisms" [1990, p. 19]. The essentially embedded information-processor which exploits redundancy of information in the environment in generating behavior that is systematic with respect to the distal states of the world is neither too occult nor too reductive, but just right.

---

are trying to explain is why bodily movements occur. It is not . . . epiphenomenal if what we are trying to explain is . . . why this or that movement is being caused to occur" [Dretske 1990, p. 12].

10.4. The Semantics of Sensation

The intentionality of states that are the paradigms of conscious accessibility—like *sensations*—are particularly common examples to focus on in encouraging internalist intuitions about intentionality. The phenomenalist construction of everything from "sense-data" was of course built around just this idea. But even here, the internalist inclinations are on shaky ground. To help show this, let me take a look at one contemporary argument about the semantics of sensation and sensation terms. Paul Churchland argues in *Scientific Realism and the Plasticity of Mind* [Churchland 1979] that the meanings of sensation terms are determined by their conceptual roles—by the ways they figure in the inferential scheme of the subject's beliefs and desires—rather than by their raw qualitative character—by the character of the kind of "raw feel" or "quale" associated with it.

But by placing the subject's own "network of beliefs" and "correlative pattern of inferences" at the basis of the semantics of sensation terms (as well as other terms, of course—more on this later), Churchland in the end aligns himself *with* the "qualitative character" account in sharing a kind of *internalism* about the semantics of sensation. It's this commitment that I take to be the deep error in both accounts, and my goal here will be to bring that out. I'll do so by turning Churchland's argument against him to show that an *information-theoretic* account—which focuses on the sensation's role with respect to the properties in the environment whose presence it signals—more adequately captures the semantics of sensation.

Churchland's argument rests entirely on the use of one particular thought-experiment in which we are asked to imagine a race of beings who perceive heat *visually*. Their eyes, unlike ours, are sensitive to the infrared spectrum. What we might think of as the "qualitative brightness" of visual experiences is then for them a function of the *temperature* of the (distal) perceptual object rather than (as for us) a function of the object's reflectivity. These beings have no color vocabulary, but use what we think of as temperature vocabulary in the following way: Their word "cold" is linked to cold objects and the sensations they get from them; but those sensations are qualitatively like those we get by looking at *dark* objects (and *mutatis mutandis* for "hot" and shadings of warmth). The world looks to them roughly the way a black and white print of an infrared film looks to us. As Churchland suggests, it seems extremely natural to say of these beings that they visually perceive the temperatures of objects.

Now on the "qualitative character" view of the semantics of sensation, their "cold" and "hot" really mean the same thing as, respectively, our "black" and "white." After all, their "cold" and our "black" are linked to the same qualitative character—the same janglings in the visual cortex, if you like. But this has the bizarre result of making their perceptual judgments systematically *false*. Since their word "cold" should mean the same thing as our word "black," "Ice cubes are cold" is *false* when uttered by one of them.

But ice cubes produce in them the sensation that they link to the word "cold." So this translation scheme for their sensation terms makes their specific and general beliefs systematically false.[3] All of this is taken as making translation based on sameness of intrinsic sensation character absurd; Churchland concludes that the intrinsic character account "must be rejected outright" [Churchland 1979, p. 13].

But the translation scheme that makes sameness of meaning a matter of sameness of overall conceptual role has no such problem, since "cold" and "hot" play roughly the same conceptual role for them as for us: They believe that ice is cold and keeps food from going bad; and that (black) ovens are hot and cause cakes to bake. This prompts Churchland to suggest that "we are left with networks of belief as the bearer or determinants of understanding" [Churchland 1979, p. 13].

10.5. Information and Sensation

But this inference should be rejected. The only motivation given for this last step is that it is compatible with the analysis of the thought experiment, in that it assigns meaning to sensation terms in such a way that the aliens don't turn out to be ridiculously and systematically wrong. But this is *not* the only account that fits the analysis of the example. If instead we take sensation terms to have the same meaning just in case they are linked to sensations that

3. Note that on this view, it's not clear why *we* shouldn't be the ones who are systematically wrong. Why shouldn't our "dark" visual experiences *really* pick out *cold* things rather than dark ones? See Putnam [1981, chap. 1] for a discussion of the absurdity here and its tie to "magical" theories of reference.

signal the presence of the same distal property in the world—that is, sensations that carry the same information about the world—we also get the non-absurd (homophonic) translation scheme.

The two accounts give the same translation scheme in the original thought experiment. To find some other way to tease them apart, we need to look at a case where sensation terms have the same general conceptual position, but where the associated sensation carries different information about the distal environment in two situations. This difference in information carried should, by the same logic as in the original example, lead us to translate in accordance with the informational properties rather than in accordance with sameness of conceptual role.

So imagine an example like the first, but where the beings differ from us in the following two ways. First, they live in an environment that has its colorations reversed with respect to ours—or to make things simple, just green and red: Things look just like they do here except that "grass" is red, "roses" are green, and so on. Second, the environment's inhabitants are built just like us, except that the normal pattern of connection between the retinal cones and the optic nerve is slightly different in them—in fact, different in exactly the way that makes the color inversions in their world, to put it a bit misleadingly, righted: When one of them looks at his (green) roses, he has exactly the same type of neural pattern received by the brain from the eyes as one of us would have upon looking at our (red) roses. If you like, they can even speak a language that is just like English, and even appropriately utter statements like "Roses are red" and "Green means go."[4]

In this new example, the inverted environment and inverted connections in the visual system have manipulated the brain-to-world relationship so that brain states with the same conceptual position as the ones we get from looking at *red* things are actually signalling the presence of *green* in the environment when they occur in our aliens' brains. They call their (green) stop signs "red," say "red"

4. The facts about color vision make this almost plausible. There are three different kinds of cones on the human retina—roughly red, green, and blue. The basic "red" and "green" detectors are physiologically distinct, and so could actually have their connections to the optic nerve crossed. In fact, since the frequencies of peak sensitivity of "red" and "green" cones are quite close to each other compared to the distance of each from the "blue" cones, the brain's determination of color as a "three-part chord" composed of these three signals won't be seriously disturbed in our example.

when shown a green object and asked what color it is, and associate with that word "red" the same "raw feel" as we associate with the word "red."

We now have exactly the same reasons for translating their "red" as "green" as we did for accepting the homophonic translation scheme in the earlier example. Their stops signs are *green*; when they say "Our stop signs are red" we'd clearly better take their use of "red" to be translated as our word "green" if they're not going to be ridiculously and systematically wrong. If we get together, and have only one red and one green Life Saver left, a major breach of interplanetary etiquette can be easily avoided if we just keep in mind that we can both say "I want the red one" and still both get exactly what we want without conflict. We thus have an example where the conceptual role (and "raw feels") translations give us schemes that leave these aliens absurdly wrong—exactly the sort of situation that led Churchland to damn the intrinsic character view initially and replace it with the conceptual role view. However strong his argument against the intrinsic character view is, we now have an equally strong argument against the conceptual role view.

The informational account of the semantics of sensation is the one that has been left standing in our battle of the translation schemes. But deeper and more systematic reasons for favoring this account come from its fit with the general embedded conception of mind that has been put forth here. Most obvious is the tie with the theory of reference and meaning discussed in chapter 8. This account of the semantics of sensation follows the same general principle of making meaning depend most centrally on what property in the world is signalled (and so in turn, referred to). It's not some local, non-relational fact about the brain state of the subject that's most central to determining the meaning of sensation terms—e.g., the "raw feel" of the associated sensation, or the term's position in the conceptual web. Rather, what's most critical are the sensation's properties *as a signal carrying information about the external environment.*[5]

5. Note that unlike the standard "Twin Earth" case using indexicals or natural-kind terms, the differences in content between "internally identical" sensations show up in differences in behavior *even when the organism is put in exactly the same context.* This gives an example where content *as it plays a role in the explanation of behavior* can differ between cases of type-identical brain states, even without using the level-relativity of context-dependence discussed in chapter 2.

10.6. From Symbol-grounding to Subjectivity

In the general area of the philosophical foundations of artificial intelligence, no issue involving intentionality has received more attention and discussion than the "symbol-grounding problem." John Searle's "Mind, Brains, and Programs" [Searle 1980] has been at the center of much of that discussion. Searle takes his central point in this article to be the refutation of what he calls "strong AI": the view that having a mind (intelligence, beliefs, etc.) is just a matter of engaging in a particular kind of activity that can be "defined in terms of computational operations on purely formally defined elements." Most centrally, it is the issue of *content* on which his position rests. As he puts it, at least some mental states are *intrinsically intentional*; but "formal symbol manipulations by themselves don't have any intentionality; they are quite meaningless; they aren't even *symbol* manipulations, since the symbols don't symbolize anything. In the linguistic jargon, they have a syntax but no semantics" [Searle 1980, p. 442].

It's not uncommon to suggest in this context that mental symbols get their interpretation from their causal interactions with the outside world. As William Lycan puts it: " . . . no computer has or could have intentional states *merely in virtue of performing syntactic operations on formally characterized elements* . . . . The content of a mental representation is not determined within the owner's head; rather, it is determined in part by the objects in the environment that actually figure in the representation's etiology and in part by social and contextual factors of several other sorts" [Lycan 1980, p. 435]. But Searle insists repeatedly that the intentional properties of thought must be "intrinsic," and thus not in this way context-dependent. This is what he calls the "intrinsic intentionality" of the symbol, and it depends for him centrally on the underlying biochemistry of the brain.

This is one natural way of taking the challenge offered by the "symbol-grounding" problem. But taken in this way, the problem is both easier to answer and more narrowly philosophical than it might be. The heart of the position is simply an insistence that there must be some "intrinsic" features of mental symbols that fill them out in such a way so as to determine their meaning—that is, for example, that the symbols have a distinctive conceptual role, and that meaning is determined by conceptual role. But not only is the appeal to intuitions about "intrinsic intentionality" close to the surface and defeasible, but arguments like the one I gave against Churchland's view of the semantics of sensation are exactly the thing to show that the intentionality of even the most phenomenologically salient and accessible of states of real brains depend on their relationship to an environment—and thus the information that they carry—for their meaning.

But there is another way to understand the "symbol-grounding" problem that gives it considerably more force, and which the main theme of this book can quite naturally be seen as providing some support for. David Kirsh [1991, p. 3] asks the central question succinctly: The real issue is whether "cognition can be studied as a disembodied process without solving the symbol-grounding problem." Can cognition be studied independently of the mechanisms by which the symbols get their semantic properties from the surrounding world; i.e., does the implementation of the embodiment of those symbols play a critical role in studying the logic or the process of the symbols themselves? On this way of taking the problem the central points of this book have a good deal to say about it.

Seeing the possibilities I've suggested for multiple paths of causation and mechanism that go into the emergence of the systematicity of embedded and interactive cognition suggests something important about at least the process account of cognition: To the extent to which cognition is critically dependent on the detail of perceptual interaction with the environment, filling in those processes and the environment they face will be an unavoidable and non-independent component of giving any reasonable theory of cognition. In this way, the detailed interactivity with the environment that specifies the information carried in perception—and in at least some sense, "grounds the symbols"—illustrates an important way in which it's fundamentally misleading to "study cognition as a disembodied process without solving the symbol-grounding problem" [Ibid.].

In spite of all this, there's still a common inclination to think that there is some clear sense of "purely inner" content: The sense in which the content of our thoughts depends only on the intrinsic character of our conscious experience—on, if you like, our phenomenology. Accepting some notion of the supervenience of the mental on the physical, the intrinsic character of these conscious experiences is entirely determined by the biophysical character of the underlying brain states. It's this phenomenological sense of "content" that is typically assumed to supervene on brain state alone, and to thus underlie the sort of meaning that is truly "in the head."

This is, I think, a pervasive (if not always explicit) suggestion. It's the sort of view that underlies perhaps the central epistemological science-fiction of latter twentieth-century philosophy—the "brain in a vat" cases. It is also sometimes found at the heart of anti-AI inclinations, as providing a kind of intrinsic inner content that is seen as supervening on the biological properties of our brains but not their information-processing properties. (See the discussion of "intrinsic intentionality" in Searle 1980.)

Of course the general theme underlying the present discussion— both in this chapter and in the book at large—might be taken to suggest something quite different: That the characterization of our mental states as *meaning-bearing* states is *essentially* dependent on their embedding in the world. Twin-Earth cases provide a kind of distortion of reference that shows that we must take into account a mind's embedding in the world in order to correctly make sense of the reference and truth values of its thoughts. The case at hand provides a kind of distortion of meaning that extends into the role that mental content has in the explanation of the intentions of agents and their relationship to behavior—to our psychology, not "just" our semantics. The importance of embedding in the world for the understanding of representational states extends not just to cases where there is some explicit division of labor, or grossly flawed knowledge of the essence of a type, but to those representational states that have long been the paradigms of direct, non-social, and reliable knowledge.

So underlying the discussion in this chapter of intentionality and embeddedness, I think there is a fundamental tension between the intentional and something like an intuition of the *subjective* or *phenomenological* character of mind. After all, even if the semantic conception of mind relies inescapably on its embedded nature, surely there is some notion of the subjective nature of the mental which does not, and for which the fundamental Cartesian intuition should still hold. In the final two chapters, I will take a look at the place of subjectivity and the phenomenological within the conception of mind I've been filling out along the way.

CHAPTER
ELEVEN

THE AUTONOMY
OF SUBJECTIVITY

Nothing encourages internalist intuitions more than thinking about the idea of *subjectivity*. Whatever we might need to say about taxonomies for the explanation of behavior, the interactivity of processing, or the semantics of mental states, the realm of the subjective character of experience is where the Cartesian intuition stands tallest. Having now set out much of the account of embedded cognition, it's to this area I'll now turn.

In this chapter, I'll consider the role that the allegedly "perspectival" nature of phenomenological properties might have with respect to the more general framework of pluralistic materialism within which I've been working, and then turn more explicitly to considering the relevance of embeddedness in this domain in the final chapter. I'll focus here on two prominent and conflicting characterizations of the place of subjectivity: Thomas Nagel's, which takes such properties to be in some sense incompatible with the materialist outlook, and William Lycan's, which takes them to be objectively identifiable and thus entirely unproblematic. I'll suggest in the end that we should take something away from both accounts, but also that both err in suggesting a kind of incompatibility between generic materialism and the idea of intrinsically phenomenological properties.

For many, Nagel's "What Is It Like to Be a Bat?" [Nagel 1979] has codified the central intuition that no objective account of mind could adequately capture subjective phenomena. But Nagel's view has suffered many attacks, notably including Lycan's recent volley [Lycan 1988]. But I believe attacks like his have overstated the case against Nagel. In explaining the ways in which the criticism fails, I'll suggest that the most important point of a position like Nagel's is its anti-*reductionism* about the subjective rather than any kind of anti-*materialism*. I will then examine what kind of irreducible or autonomous subjectivity might actually be possible even within a materialist framework.

11.1. Nagel's Point of View

Most centrally, Nagel presents a conception of subjectivity which seems to many to capture something at the heart of the idea of an *irreducibly subjective character of experience.* As he puts it, "an organism has conscious mental states if and only if there is something it is like to *be* that organism—something it is like *for* the organism" [Nagel 1979, p. 166]. And it is this notion of subjectivity which he thinks stands squarely in the way of providing an objectifying (or "reductive") analysis of mind. He suggests that we have no way of seeing how such an analysis is even *possible,* since "any reductionist program has to be based on an analysis of what is to be reduced . . . . Without some idea, therefore, of what the subjective character of experience is, we cannot know what is required of physicalist theory" [Nagel 1979, p. 71]. And further, if an objective analysis of mind must account for the subjective character of experience, "we must admit that no presently available conception gives us a clue how this could be done" [Nagel 1979, p. 175]. That is, we don't only lack a particular account of the mind-body relationship that can account for subjectivity; we furthermore lack an answer even to the question of how such a thing might be possible—we lack even any kind of *schema* for an answer. But what would it be to have such a schema, if the traditional answers to the mind-body question—e.g., behaviorism, functionalism, physicalism, etc.—don't count as giving one? What is it to "leave out" subjectivity?

Nagel does not rely on what I see as the most standard way to support an anti-materialist (or anti-functionalist) line here—although he doesn't hesitate to advocate it along the way. This is the standard "zombie" illustration: Subjectivity is "not captured by any of the familiar, recently-devised reductive analyses of the mental, for *all of them are logically compatible with its absence of subjective character of experience.* It is not analyzable in terms of any explanatory system of functional states, or intentional states, since they could be ascribed to robots or automata that behaved like people though they experienced nothing" [Nagel 1979, pp. 166–167]. This answer has surely been around forever[1] and it

---

1. Consider, for example, Leibniz's version from *The Monadology*: " . . . *perception* and that which depends on it are *inexplicable by mechanical causes.* . . . Supposing that there were a machine so constructed as to think, feel and have perception, we could conceive of it as enlarged and yet preserving the same proportions, so that we might enter it as into a mill. And this granted, we should only find on visiting

never really goes totally out of style. But it has seemed especially popular—at least as a subject of debate—over the last 20 years or so. John Searle's infamous "Chinese room" example [Searle 1980] and the various anti-functionalist homunculi-head examples [see Block 1978] are among the better-known of these. But the problems with this line are well-known. Most importantly, the intuition that the standard simulations of human structure *don't* have mentality, intentionality, subjectivity, or whatever it is that you want is not one that we all find so completely compelling. After all, if you weren't already pretty sure about the subjectivity lurking within human brains, you'd likely be pretty skeptical that this rumpled lump of hydrocarbons is what turns the cosmic trick.

Why is it *subjectivity* that's so hard to capture? The heart of Nagel's suggestion is that "every subjective phenomenon is essentially connected with a single point of view, and it seems inevitable that an objective, physical theory will abandon that point of view" [Nagel 1979, p. 167]. Subjectivity is essentially tied to this idea of a point of view, but any objective analysis must leave that behind. There are facts (about "what it's like") which "embody" and "are accessible only from" [Nagel 1979, p. 163] a particular point of view, and hence "cannot be captured by any objective reduction." So, for example, we can't imagine what it's like to be a bat, and to perceive by bat sonar, even though we might well think that they have some subjective character of experience. Or as just the same idea was put by an earlier advocate of a focus on the phenomenological: "A man born deaf knows that there are sounds, that sounds produce harmonies and that a splendid art depends upon them. But he cannot understand *how* sounds do this, how musical compositions are possible. Such things he cannot *imagine*, i.e., he cannot "see" and in "seeing" grasp the "how" of such things" [Husserl 1964, pp. 3–4].

11.2. Lycan's Responses

In his reply to Nagel [Lycan 1988, chap. 7], Lycan allows that there is a natural reading of Nagel's point which is quite correct. He readily acknowledges that "seeing someone's brain in a state of sensing-blazing-red is nothing at all like sensing blazing red oneself" [p. 76]. And similarly with respect to the bat's sonar sensation

---

it, pieces which push one against another, but never anything by which to explain a perception" [1962, p. 206].

S: "We do not know what it is like to have *S* (we do not have cognitive access to *S*) *in the way the bat does*."

But these facts are "welcomed by the materialist" [p. 77]. When I observe the bat in some physical or functional state, I don't thereby *have* that state myself, and I don't have the same perspective with respect to it. But a materialist account of the mental should not claim otherwise; as he puts it, "the felt incongruity is just what anyone, materialist or anti-materialist alike, should expect. Therefore the incongruity affords no objection whatever to materialism" [ibid.]. The feeling of profound incongruity between *having* the state and *knowing from the outside about it* is a natural and expectable consequence of the fact that the two involve—to adopt the functionalist/computationalist form—representing the event in entirely distinct representational formats. As Paul Churchland [1984, p. 34] puts essentially the same point: The critical difference "may reside not in *what* is respectively known by each (brain states by the former, nonphysical *qualia* by the latter), but rather in the different *type*, or *medium*, or *level* of representation each has of exactly the same thing."

This "functional" reply (as Lycan calls it) thus aims to *defuse* rather than *refute* the intuition of incongruity, and is quite plausible when directed against one common way of taking Nagel's claim. Suggesting that there are constraints and limits on the character of our representation of stimuli hardly constitutes giving an argument against (in particular, a roughly functionalist) materialism. Such limitations are *exactly* what one would expect on the functionalist or materialist account, and so should hardly count against them. There are ways of knowing or "grasping" you can't engage in without the right perspective, but this should not be seen as impugning materialism or functionalism.

But this does not completely dispose of Nagel's claim, and Lycan quite rightly sees this. He acknowledges a second possible kind of essentially "non-objective" or "perspectival" facts—facts that can only be *referred to* by making use of the appropriate subjective perspective. The challenge provided here is in my view more problematic; and Lycan's arguments against it less watertight.

According to Lycan, "we can suppose that [the fact's] alleged perspectivalness is located either in an individual constituent or in a property constituent" [Lycan 1988, p. 79]. For the sake of clarity, let me focus on the latter case. What would it be for a fact to have an intrinsically perspectival property as constituent? On Lycan's view, this amounts to claiming that "there is [a property] concept that can be grasped and/or reported only in a first-person, perspectival way, and not in the third-person, objective way" [Lycan 1988, p. 79]. But such a concept is a "function from worlds to sets of individuals" as he sees it; and he insists that *any such function is objectively describable*, or so it would seem . . . " [ibid.]. The problem then is that "It seems Nagel will have to eschew this powerful and effective way of representing the constituents of propositions and facts if he is to maintain the existence of perspectival ones, and that we should be loath to do" [ibid.].

Now on the whole, I'm significantly less loath to give up the "power and effectiveness" of possible worlds semantics than Lycan is. More "situated" accounts of the semantics of propositions (like *situation semantics* [Barwise and Perry 1983]) aren't just to be ruled out; in chapter 8, I've looked a little way down that path. But even within this perspective, the argument here doesn't do the job.

What is it to claim that there will be, for any allegedly perspectival property, an "objectively describable" or "not intrinsically perspectival" function from worlds to sets of individuals? Lycan's gloss on the notion is slightly puzzling: " . . . there is nothing intrinsically perspectival about functions from worlds to individuals; any one could be described by anyone who had the right sort of mental apparatus or brain writing" [Lycan 1988, p. 79]. But if this is what "objective" amounts to here, it's not clear how it answers Nagel at all. Nagel's claim was that there are facts such that knowledge of them (or perhaps even reference to their constituents) requires making use of a particular sort of perspective—such as that of being constituted in a certain way. If the sense in which the "function" is objectively describable is just that *anybody constituted in the right way* can characterize it, then no rebuttal has been given to the claim that no objective theory can characterize the facts about bat phenomenology so that they can be referred to by beings (like us) who don't share the bat's structure and perspective.

Part of the confusion here may come from Lycan's implicit dichotomy between reporting in a "first-person, perspectival" way and in a "third-person, objective" way. Nagel quite rightly allows that we might refer in the third person to intrinsically perspectival facts that we don't stand in exactly the right first-person relationship to—as when I refer to your pains, or to Wade Boggs' perception of a curve ball. I'm surely doing so in some kind of mediate way—by making critical use of someone *else's* perspective. But referring to the subjective state through the reports and authority of the subject hardly makes them non-subjective; I refer to them then in a third-person but still perspectival way.[2]

Furthermore, as I discussed in chapter 8, it's now an entirely ubiquitous suggestion that what we refer to is conditioned by the environmental context in which our thoughts and utterances occur. What fixes the reference of our words and thoughts isn't just "in the head," but in the structures of the physical world and social context around us. By making use of the context, there may be all sorts of ways to refer to features of the character of experience of beings other than ourselves. The constituents of "funny facts" needn't be entirely inaccessible in order for them to be undescribable in the language of any particular functional account of the mental.

11.3. Autonomy Again

But the problems involved in resisting "perspectival facts" go even deeper than this. Not only does Lycan's own argument fail, but there are also substantive reasons from within the philosophy of science which would seem to support at least some aspect of Nagel's claim.

Consider the standard functionalist reply to more reductive versions of materialism—a move which Lycan not only endorses, but characterizes as "the only positive doctrine in all of philosophy that I am prepared (if not licensed) to kill for" [1988, p. 37]. The standard token physicalist account of materialism that goes hand-in-hand with functionalism is motivated first and foremost by the sense that higher-level properties of systems—functional properties, if you like—are not definable in physical terms. The moral here is now commonplace, and should be clear from the discussions in part I: Token physicalism does not require *property* identity between the higher-level and the lower-level—in this case, the mental and the physical. Multiple realizability and context-dependence counter definability; and this fundamental irreducibility makes the presence of higher-level sciences not just an accident of local epistemology, but a basic part of carving the world at its joints. As before: To be a

2. Nagel of course does not think subjective properties are essentially private, just that constraints on one's mental life can make some *types* of them inaccessible. We can perfectly well, on his view, imagine what it's like to be another human who is sufficiently like we are—a friend, maybe even the vice-president [see Nagel 1979, pp. 171–172].

gene, or a gene of a particular type, is not the same thing as being a DNA molecule of a particular type. They are not identical *properties*, although states of affairs in the world consisting in something being a gene of a certain type are also states of affairs consisting in something being a DNA molecule of a certain type.

This suggests that if we were to count facts as distinct when they have distinct *property* constituents, then the fact that's known when you know that something is an instance of C-fiber stimulation and the fact that's known when you know something is an instance of pain are different facts. Lycan has claimed—quite reasonably, as I've said—that the "functional" account of "perspectival facts" doesn't make any headway against materialism or functionalism since the restrictions on knowledge generated are just what the materialist or functionalist should have expected, and in no way conflicts with the view. But this case is different. In this case, the problem is not just that knowing the imagined functional account doesn't mean knowing what the experience is like from the standpoint of the experiencer; it's that knowing the functional account may not even facilitate *reference* to the experiential properties *as those kinds of phenomenological properties*—just as physical descriptions don't pick out functional properties *as such*.

What is needed to refer to phenomenological *properties* as such in objective terms? Referring to the brain states that are token identical with the phenomenological events or states is not enough to accomplish picking out the appropriate phenomenological properties as such. After all, it's not adequate for picking out the properties of the system at the functional or computational level either—that is the central point of the ubiquitous advocacies of token over type physicalism. Computational properties are essentially undefinable in the language of physics, or neurophysiology, for that matter. The reference to the property at the appropriate level has to organize and taxonomize it correctly. But it is simply an open possibility that no theory will do this. No physical theory of the brain will allow the picking out of computational properties as such; in the same way, it may well turn out that no computational account of the mind's working will allow defining the phenomenological properties of the brain as such.

The possibility for the autonomy of the phenomenological which I've illustrated here, although not in the end anti-*materialist*, is strongly enough anti-*reductionist* to be of some concern to mainstream physicalists (like Churchland) and functionalists (like

Lycan). On this possibility, the irreducibility of the subjective would be due, not to some general anti-materialism, but to the possible anomalousness of the phenomenological with respect to the computational. But then I don't think that anomalousness and autonomy between explanatory accounts should *ever* be seen as particularly surprising. Rather, it's the converse which should surprise us when it turns out to be the case. The relationship between higher-level and lower-level properties of complex systems is not just in *principle* multiple realizability; we may often find multiple realization of higher-level properties within the very same structure, and even multiple realization of the very same token higher-level entity.

This is particularly so when we enter domains in which something like a computational account of activity starts to seem appealing—as it does here for Lycan. The implementation of higher-level primitives in computer programs provides a particularly clear example of the possibilities of multiple realizability even *within* a particular complex system, as in the case of variable implementation given at the end of chapter 1. There, the implementations of the higher-level primitive were an important and interesting class only via their unified role at the higher level of organization. And this sort of phenomenon is also particularly ubiquitous in the social domains. An individual's wealth, a baseball team, a corporation, a story—all are cases where the identity of token and how it instantiates some higher-level property can vary dramatically in the details of its lower-level implementation over time. The process of change and identity is determined by the rules of the game at the higher rather than the lower level of organization.

As I discussed in chapter 3, these sorts of cases typically have two different features preventing the mapping between levels: *multiple realizability* allows different lower-level structures to implement the same higher-level feature, and *context-dependence* allows the very same lower-level structure to implement different higher-level objects in different contexts. Furthermore, it's not only that exactly the same properties of some local device can contribute differently to the overall functioning of a complex system (as, when the same air flow control properties locally could be either functionally a choke or a throttle). The interplay between levels and context-dependence will also allow higher-level facts about context to make the same local part play different functional roles *because they make different properties of that local part functionally salient* (as in the case of the switching transistor discussed at the end of chap. 1).

Similarly in the current case: The context of the phenomenological may determine that different aspects of the lower-level activity of the brain become salient in the organism's phenomenology than those which matter to the computational structure of that brain. Different details may be left behind as noise, and different patterns made significant as generalities—as was the case for the two roles for the transistor. The degree to which computationalist accounts "hide" much of the process and representation from consciousness already indicates that the computational outlook takes as significant various processes and patterns which are not salient in the phenomenology. We have been given no good reason to suppose that the inverse is not true as well.

11.4. A Middle Ground

The moral for the idea of a phenomenological-to-computational property identification is clear. Any such suggested account faces the problematic possibility that phenomenological properties are multiply realizable by various computational states which have no particular computational properties in common; the possibility that the very same computational states will underlie different experiences, depending on their position in the more global functioning of the organism; and—most importantly, I think—the possibility that a phenomenological rather than a computational context will make different aspects of the total lower-level swarm of detail functionally significant rather than just bits of noise. With this stack of possibilities running against you, it hardly seems far-fetched to suggest that you *might* fail.

This kind of suggestion would then seem to leave Nagel half right, at least. Lycan (and Churchland) fail to rule out the possibility that subjectivity is uncharacterizable except from the perspective of the subject (or one suitably similar, whatever that comes to in the end). It is having that perspective or point of view that allows for our normal ability to refer to those phenomenological properties *as such*. Whether other contexts will allow independent paths for referring to those same properties remains an unanswered question. But even if it turns out that there is no objective characterization of subjective facts or properties as such, and that any such properties *are* importantly perspective-bound, this shouldn't be viewed at all as being anti-*materialist*. Non-reductive identity materialism explicitly *claims* that not all properties are physical properties; that's what distinguishes it from the more reductive accounts.

But this *would* conflict with a functionalist or computationalist view which suggests that subjective mental *properties* (and not just individual mental *states* or *events*) are *identifiable with* (and not just supervenient on) some kind of more "scientifically respectable" properties (e.g., computational or biological properties). This allows for the possibility of a much deeper limitation on functionalist accounts than that suggested by Lycan's "functional" reply to Nagel. His point was just that *knowing* the functionalist account of some subjective state didn't thereby allow you to "know what it's like" to have the state; the "different formats" response seems to me entirely reasonable. But now the problem is that knowing the functional account may not even facilitate *reference* to the phenomenological properties at all, in that the phenomenological properties may not be characterizable in functionalist terms—just as computational properties are not characterizable in physical terms.

So on the one hand, I've argued that Lycan's criticism of Nagel's claim that subjectivity is essentially irreducible doesn't do the job. But I've also suggested that the coherent model that can be provided for essentially irreducible phenomenological properties doesn't impugn materialism in any of its less reductive forms at all. So in a sense, I'm actually disagreeing with both of them. Nagel and Lycan both see the possibility of some kind of intrinsically phenomenological properties as being in conflict with materialism, but then differ in whether there might be such properties. But I've suggested that nothing like anti-materialism follows from such an idea. Intrinsically perspectival (phenomenological) properties don't require anything more than the kind of anomalous monism that motivates the non-reductive conception of function within the materialist framework.

Furthermore, both Nagel and Lycan are committed to an explicit position under the current state of the evidence about whether there actually *are* any intrinsically perspectival properties (i.e., phenomenological properties which aren't in any sense reducible to any other kind of properties). In contrast, the position I've argued for takes an explicitly agnostic position on this. Whether there are irreducibly perspectival properties or not is for me (unlike them) an open question which is post-theoretical rather than pre-theoretical in nature.

The main thrust of this chapter has been to argue that a failure to *reduce* the phenomenological to the functional or computational shouldn't commit you to any kind of anti-materialist view. An identification of phenomenological properties with computational ones is too strong a constraint to place on the kind of pluralistic token materialism assumed by functionalist views in the first place. Even if phenomenological properties globally supervene on computational ones, they needn't be identifiable with particular computationally characterizable properties. Phenomenological characterizations may well specify coarser-grained properties of the system's activity, exhibiting the kind of multiple realizability and context-dependence with respect to the computational which are the marks of autonomous levels of organization. In the next and final chapter, I'll turn return more explicitly to embeddedness, and consider its bearing on the autonomy of the phenomenological.

EXISTENTIAL
COGNITION

We've moved our informational analysis of mind now to a consideration of the phenomenological. I won't try to go too far down this path here; that's another project. But when in Rome, maybe it's worth at least checking out what the Romans have been up to. So in conclusion, I'll take a brief look at a few of the connections to be made here, and suggest some possible directions to take them.

There are three critical ideas to be taken from the phenomenological outlook here that I think will shed important light on the current discussion. One is the distinction between the *real* and the *intentional* aspects of mental acts—as Husserl names them, *noesis* and *noema*. The second is the notion of phenomenological *bracketing*, a methodological strategy for separating thought and world. And the third is the idea of the *existential* turn in phenomenology, where the essences of mental acts are taken as *transcendent* (i.e., dependent on factors outside of the experience itself) as opposed to *immanent*.

12.1. The Syntax of Consciousness

What could a computational theory of consciousness be like? How could it turn out that phenomenological properties *are* computational after all? There is a suggestion about consciousness that is fairly obvious once one takes up the information-processing outlook: The character of conscious experience is a matter of the syntactic or formal properties of some particular class of representations tokened in the process of mental activity—perhaps those in some central short-term working space [as in Dennett 1978], or those used in some particular high-level control loop [Johnson-Laird 1983]. Or as Ray Jackendoff puts it, "The elements of conscious awareness are caused by/supported by/projected from information and processes of the computational mind" [Jackendoff 1987, p. 23].

Let's take a brief look at what I think is a relatively representative "syntactic" account of consciousness—Ray Jackendoff's, from *Consciousness and the Computational Mind* [1987]—and suggest how the general approach has presuppositions that we are now in a position to question—with a little help from the phenomenological distinction between *noesis* and *noema*.

It's important to note the degree to which views like these take the phenomenological to depend on the computational. Phenomenological distinctions must be computational distinctions. It's not enough that there simply be a relationship of bare supervenience. In this way they are like Lycan's view discussed in the last chapter. As Jackendoff puts it, "If there is a phenomenological distinction not yet expressed by our current computational theory, the theory must be enriched or revised" [1987, p. 25]. In this way, "we will seek to explain the elements of the computational mind and their causal interactions in those terms disallowing explanations in the terms of phenomenological causation" [p. 26].

Jackendoff's real worry here is that "without a coherent notion of what could possibly be meant by phenomenological causation, this kind of argument amounts essentially to an appeal to magic" [ibid. p. 26]. But much of the preceding discussion in this book has suggested what mental causation above the level of the computational might amount to. There are no appeals to magic; only to the essential embedding of the organism in its environment. Jackendoff sees no option for explaining the activities of the mind other than the physical or computational options. The option of mental process as an embedded and interactive process taking place at a level of organization higher than that of the computational is not one he sees.

The parallels to Fodor's "methodological solipsism" are clear: The central suggestion is that distinctions in the canonical taxonomy for phenomenological states (as for *intentional* states, on Fodor's account) are coextensive with (or at least isomorphic with) some set of distinctions in the information-processing characterization of the human cognitive system. Or to put it another way: the phenomenological *reduces* (methodologically, at least) to the computational.

There's also a particular *form* of this "reduction" that's often implied, and Jackendoff makes it quite explicit in what he calls "Lashley's conjecture": the view that "computational activity—processing—is always unconscious: what is revealed to consciousness is the consequence of processing, namely an information structure . . . only structures, not processes, support distinctions in awareness" [pp. 45–46].

But the methodological assumption that phenomenological distinctions are format distinctions isn't justified—partly for reasons I went through in chapter 11. Even if the phenomenological globally supervenes on the computational,[1] phenomenological properties needn't be coextensive with local syntactic properties of representations. Phenomenological properties could be context-dependent properties of those representations, or could be properties of groups, streams, or processes defined over representations that might be multiply realizable at the level of real token syntactic objects—that is, they might well be an irreducible higher level of organization of the system.

To fill this possibility out more, it will be helpful to turn to one of the critical distinctions that I'll borrow from real phenomenology: Husserl's distinction between *noesis* and *noema*.

12.2. Noesis and Noema

One distinction in phenomenology that clearly runs back to its founding is Husserl's distinction between *noeses*—the real temporal parts (or "proper components") of an experience—and *noema*—an act's essential *intentional* character (or "correlate"). On the *noetic* side of the analysis of experience we have "the parts and phases which we find through a *real (reele) analysis* of the experience in which we treat the experience as an object like any other, and question it concerning its parts or the dependent phases which build it up on real (*reell*) lines" [Husserl 1964, p. 237]. Noeses are real temporal components of experience; they are "animating apprehensions" that "belong to the real (*reellen*) constitution of the experience" [p. 362].

But on the *noematic* side "the intentional experience is the consciousness of something, and is so in the form its essence prescribes" [p. 237]. This noema, the "perceived as such", is not a real part of the act; it "is as little contained *realiter (reell)* in the perception as is the tree of the real natural order" [p. 261]; it "belongs to the experience in a completely different sense from that in which the real (reellen) and consequently proper constituents of the experience belong to it"

1. I'll examine the possibility that it doesn't supervene later in the chapter.

[p. 263]. In fact, this "completely different sense" is different enough to push the "existential" phenomenologist to break the connection and deny that the intentional essence here belongs to the experience independently of its embedding in the world. But for Husserl, the noema is "not affected by the suspending of the reality"; it "does indeed belong to the essence of the perceptual experience in itself" [p. 261].

Husserl's noema is an essentially intentional entity; as he says, a generalization of the notion of *Sinn* [p. 238], or Fregean sense. It is a part of the intentional essence of an experience; or if you prefer, it is the experience taxonomized in terms of its directedness on the world. What unites various conscious noetic acts into a single noema for Husserl is that the various acts make up an intentional directedness toward some particular object or properties in the world perceived as such. Noematic features are presented in experience as inhering in the object, and not in the fluctuating state of the subject; they are the "object pole" as opposed to the "subject pole" of experience.

The noema also gives a more coarse-grained characterization of the experience than one in terms of noesis; the same noema can undergo significant variation over time in terms of the nature of the underlying noetic acts. For example, in considering the noematic side of the perception of color, he claims that

> the noematic or 'objective' colour 'manifests itself in varying perspectives.' But one and the same noematic colour of which we are thus aware *as* self-same, in itself unchanged within the unity of a continuously changing perceptual consciousness, runs through its perspective variations in a continuous variety of sensory colours. We see a tree unchanged in colour—its own colour as a tree— whilst the positions of the eyes, the relative orientations, change in many respects, the glance wanders ceaselessly over the trunk and branches, whilst we step nearer at the same time, and thus in different ways excite the flow of perceptual experience. [p. 261]

Taking a hint from seeing the noema as intentional correlate rather than proper part of the intentional act, we might similarly in the naturalistic case find the best account of the object-directed phenomenological state not in the unity of some particular representational state, but in the constancy of the object of the experience. The intentional or phenomenological unities in experience—the taxonomy under which human action has its noticeable systematicities as rational and goal-directed—needn't be real, temporal parts of the flow of consciousness, but might be the (abstract, intentional) noematic unities of the real noetic phases of consciousness. The shift in grain between the noetic and the noematic suggests the possibility of a parallel shift between the computational and the phenomenological that leaves the latter as fundamentally non-reducible and autonomous.

Before leaving this issue, it's worth noting that the distinction between the rapidly fluctuating noetic acts and the underlying constancy of the noema underlies a theme in the "animate" approach to vision discussed in chapter 9 as well. Given the rapid and global shifts of retinally-indexed information due to saccadic eye movements, where does the stability of the phenomenology of perception come from? As Ballard [1991, p. 83] asks the question: Since "most of the brain's structures that represent visual information are retinally indexed . . . their state is changing with each eye movement . . . . How can the world appear to be stable when the data collecting process is so dynamic? . . . the way the apparatus works at this level of abstraction . . . is very incompatible with phenomenological notions of invariance and stability."

The "illusion" of invariance and stability also might be filled out to include the idea of the "illusion" of something like *fullness*. We not only see the visual field as stable, but as full. We typically feel as though the field is all there, and we just have to turn our attention toward it. Of course, not only the facts about the uneven resolution of the retinal image but the even more mundane facts about the invisibility of your "blind spot" point out that the early-stage image is neither full nor constant in the way perception seems to be.

One natural way to take what we've seen so far is that the source of stability of the visual field is in a very strong sense the stability of the environment. The visual field is full and constant only *dispositionally*. The character of the percept depends on facts like our ability to scan the scene at will, and that the scene will remain appropriately stable across such scans. But at least this much is clear: The stability of the "veil of perception" is nothing like any stability in the proximal stimulus. The stability and fullness of perception are functions of the embeddedness of the organism.

12.3. Methodology and "Bracketing"

In the introduction, I suggested that a critical part of our task is to find the characterizations of the world under which behavior is systematic with respect to it—the ontology of the world that we must discover in order to explain our behavior in it. That is, we need to find the taxonomy or description under which we see the world, and to frame our accounts of intelligent behavior in terms of carving the world into intentional objects the way that we do. The essential project of phenomenology is essentially just this project. In trying to provide a "purely descriptive science of the intentional structure of mental acts," we are searching for the taxonomy under which we see the world.

We might have glossed the end of this by saying "the way we see the world—*for better or worse.*" And this is the essential first step in the central methodological device for Husserl's phenomenology: that of *bracketing the world.* The point isn't to worry about getting the *right* way to see the world, but just the way we *do* see it. As a first approximation, bracketing is a kind of variation on Cartesian doubt. When I *bracket* claims about the world, I "abstain" from judgement as to their truth or falsity, and only make use of those aspects of the mental act that are "immanent" or immediately given to consciousness with "apodictic certainty."

Bracketing is thus sometimes referred to as a "reduction" to what's *given.* But it's not an *ontological* reduction—i.e., an attempt to define away questions of existence and truth in terms of the immanent structures of consciousness. Rather, this kind of "reduction" is a reduction of the subject matter of a discipline—phenomenology, or phenomenological psychology—to just that which is available to reflection once all knowledge of the real, external world has been bracketed. This reduction "is a *methodological* device for 'reducing,' or narrowing down, the scope of one's inquiry" [Smith and McIntyre 1982, p. 95]. There's no guarantee that "object" or "tree" should be *definable* in terms that survive the reduction, then. Rather, the aspects of "object" or "tree" that we consider are constrained as a matter of methodology to those that survive the process of bracketing. In this way, phenomenology needn't be viewed as any kind of phenomenalism—of say, the kind that the positivists advocated.

The independence of the taxonomy of mental states from considerations involving the external world which is captured for Husserl in the notion of *bracketing* (i.e., the idea that mental states are what they are independently of what the external world is like) is for cognitivists captured in something like the idea of *methodological solipsism.* As I discussed it in chapter 2, methodological solipsism, on Fodor's account, is the supposition that psychological processes honor the *formality condition:*

> formal operations apply in terms of the, as it were, shapes of the objects in their domains [Fodor 1980, p. 227]

> . . . they have access only to the formal properties of such representations of the environment as the senses provide. Hence, they have no access to the *semantic* properties of such representations, including the property of being true, of having referents, or, indeed, the property of being representations *of the environment.* [Ibid., p. 231]

> . . . it follows that content alone cannot distinguish thoughts . . . two thoughts can be distinct in content only if they can be identified with relations to formally distinct representations. [Ibid., p. 227]

So the formality condition, like Husserl's bracketing, makes the assumption that the "external" properties of our intentional states (such as what particular real object they happen to be about, or whether or not they happen to be true) are outside the scope of what psychology should look at. As Dreyfus puts it, "this bracketing of the concerns of naturalism, along with the implicit denial of the causal component of reference, makes Husserl a methodological solipsist" [Dreyfus 1982, pp. 14–15].

Furthermore, the two views seem to share at least two central motivations for making the methodological reduction of subject matter via bracketing and the formality condition. One is the obvious one—a (tentative, anyway) acceptance of the Cartesian intuition that our mental states could have been exactly as they are regardless of the state of or even existence of the external world. And the other is a hope for a science of the mind that is in a certain sense "presuppositionless"—which for Husserl is typically taken to be the sense of something like standard epistemological foundationalism—i.e., depending on only the "indubitably given foundations" of, presumably, something like sense-data.

But for methodological solipsism, the key is to avoid presupposing other *scientific* successes.[2] After all (as discussed in chap. 8), if the meanings and extensions of at least *some* terms depend on facts

---

2. Husserl is also particularly interested in not presupposing any other *science* or body of scientific knowledge. References to the bracketing of scientific knowledge in particular appear constantly in Husserl's writings; e.g., "Thus *sciences which relate me to this natural world* . . . though I am far from any thought of objecting to them

about "hidden essences" of the things we refer to and what science can tell us about them, then (according to the post 1970's conventional wisdom) "water" refers to H_2O and "salt" refers to NaCl, whether the user knows any chemistry or not. Hence, whether a thought "water is wet" is about *water* or not "depends on whether it's about H_2O; and whether it's about H_2O depends on 'how science turns out'—viz., on what chemistry is true" [Fodor 1980, p. 247]. So if individuation of contents (and hence mental states) is done via their "external" semantic features (like their *referents*), we won't be able to type-individuate mental states without finishing up our chemistry (and presumably the rest of our sciences) first. As Fodor puts it: "No doubt it's all right to have a research strategy that says 'wait awhile.' But who wants to wait *forever*?" [p. 248]. Thus, since *not* honoring the formality condition seems to make the project of intentional psychology hopeless, all we can do is hope for a psychology that *does* honor it—one that "puts out of action" these naturalistic notions.

But we now have in hand a multiplicity of reasons for rejecting this concern. Considerations offered throughout the book support the idea that the analysis of thought should not separate it from its interactions with the environment, and that isolating it in this way will remove much of the systematicity that begs for explanation. But perhaps most importantly, as pointed out in chapter 8, although the facts about the environment that fix the referents of natural-kind terms might well be those we discover by our progress in the appropriately related science, this doesn't seem like a good model for the general case of reference fixation. More commonly the relevant facts are ones concerning perceptual relationships and social structures. But particularly in the latter case, these are hardly facts that we should wait for our science to tell us about.

Fortunately, we don't have to wait for an ideal science to pick out the objects and kinds in the world such that relations to them are intrinsic to the taxonomizing of psychological states that captures rational systematicities. We can pick them out *ourselves*. We are, clearly, terrific detectors of the intentional objects of human thought. At a first glance, we simply need to use *ourselves* as the detectors of the properties in the world relevant for the explanation of human behavior and intelligence.

---

in the least degree, *I disconnect them all . . . no one of them serves me for a foundation*" [Husserl 1964, p. 100].

This may in fact suggest that the only kind of science that will in any way characterize such facts for us will be in a certain sense an *intrinsically human science*. Recall that in chapter 11, I argued that we might still end up with some notion of irreducibly subjective properties. In this case, it might be that the basic taxonomy for the human sciences will be irreducibly subjective in at least some sense. The idea of a kind of phenomenological approach to social sciences is given a certain clear sense in this context: There might well be explanations of the behavior of complex systems (e.g., human beings in context) where the appropriate taxonomy is such that its properties can only be detected by systems suitably like those being explained; in this case, human cognitive systems. Furthermore, maybe only by those of a particular sort—like, say, the ones in that society itself.

After all, the intentional objects in the shared environment with respect to which behavior is systematic are often objects that are complex and non–physically-definable features of the world that we in fact readily detect. Such properties of the environment would include fairly low-level features like phonemes in the speech stream, or colors in natural contexts. Both are quite abstract properties of the stimuli[3] which must be pulled out of the complex environmental stimulus; vision and speech perception work in AI focuses on just such tasks. What makes these real *classes* at all has to do with their relationship to particular sorts of detectors; roughly, ones like those embodied in us. We have good detectors for these intentional objects, and can readily pick them out and sometimes even state behavioral systematicities relative to them (e.g., facts about color preferences). But "how science turns out" won't be determining the reference for representations of color and phonological feature in the way it might for "water"—that is, by discovering the hidden microphysical essence. Here, we're looking at a class that is in part defined by its relationship to human (or at least human-like) processes of perception.

12.4. Bracketing as Heuristic

We might, however, take the idea of bracketing in a different way. In contrast to the Husserlian strategy outlined above, Merleau-Ponty

3. See Nusbaum and DeGroot [1991] for a discussion of the case of phonemes; see Hardin [1988] for that of colors.

(largely in *The Phenomenology of Perception* [1962]) reconstructs the notion as one of something like a heuristic for getting us to notice certain aspects of the real, transcendent world, rather than a reduction in the epistemological, ontological, or methodological sense. This bracketing doesn't then move us away from the world; rather, for Merleau-Ponty, our experience is a "communion" with the world that cannot in the end be bracketed. Instead, bracketing encourages us—even tricks us, if you like—into refocusing our attention on the normally unthought presuppositions of thought and action in the world. As Merleau-Ponty puts it,

> It is because we are through and through compounded of relationships with the world that for us the only way to become aware of the fact is to suspend the resultant activity, to refuse it our complicity . . . or yet again, to put it 'out of play.' Not because we reject the certainties of common sense and natural attitude to things— they are, on the contrary, the constant theme of philosophy—but because, being the presupposed basis of any thought, they are taken for granted, and go unnoticed, and because in order to arouse them and bring them to view, we have to suspend for a moment our recognition of them . . . . Reflection does not withdraw from the world towards the unity of consciousness as the world's basis; it steps back to watch the forms of transcendence fly up like sparks from a fire [1962, p. xiii]

By focusing on the (often unconscious) background of presuppositions of our thought and action, Merleau-Ponty's reconstruction has the effect of transforming the idea of phenomenology somewhat—from the idea of a transcendentally purified analysis of the immediately given structures of consciousness, to something more like a reflective examination of the general structure of human directedness, and the ontology of the world that it presupposes. It is "the determination to bring the world to light as it is before any falling back on ourselves has occurred, it is the ambition to make reflection emulate the unreflective life of consciousness" [ibid., p. xvi].

We certainly needn't see the presuppositions that come out as being all that "constitutes" the object for us. There may be presuppositions that the trick of bracketing (or taking LSD, or anything else, for that matter) simply may not bring out for us—perhaps even ones that might be discovered by some science of the world. There is no guarantee of the total reliability or completeness of the deliverance of perception after bracketing.

Given this notion of bracketing, it's possible that other kinds of stances toward ourselves in the world might play the same role as that of bracketing—i.e., the role of a heuristic or trick that gets us to examine the taken-for-granted preconditions on thought and action. This "bracketing as heuristic" position opens up the possibility that one such refocus of attention we might take toward the presuppositions of our knowledge and action would be to reconceptualize the activity as (situated) computation. In this way, a phenomenological account might be naturally tied to the idea of specifying the *task content* as opposed to the *process structure* of cognition, as discussed most centrally in chapter 1. As with the other examples of task or content accounts, a phenomenological account tries to give an abstract structure of the kind of task of human activity—not a procedure for deciding what to do, but the logic of the activity that you might engage in by thinking. In Merleau-Ponty's words, "It is a matter of describing, not of explaining or analyzing" [p. viii], that "tries to give a direct description of our experience as it is, without taking account of its psychological origin and the causal explanations which the scientist, the historian or the sociologist may be able to provide" [p. vii].

The idea of bracketing-as-heuristic allows the possibility that one such stance might be to refocus on ourselves as information-processors. None of what I've said about embedding here should be taken as ruling out the possible importance of information-processing characterizations of conscious activity. In fact, some kind of information-processing account of consciousness will likely play an important part in distinguishing consciousness in terms of its role with respect to other mental states and processes. We do know some kinds of things about the role of consciousness in the overall information-processing that goes on in us. But the things that we do know fit best—I think—with the kinds of information-processing distinctions that fit well with the sort of embedded-process account that I've been advocating.

Perhaps the clearest feature of consciousness from the start is that of its being correlated with something like *attention*—a limited-capacity processor with some interesting tendencies toward flexibility, and both the strengths and the weaknesses that come with it. But notice also that many of the ways in which attention is captured at first glance characterize something like the *content* of thought. Attention is to a particular task, to a particular object, to particular properties in the world. The extent to which this might be cashed out in terms of particular representations or formats is fairly open. The ebb and flow of attention is first and foremost an activity of *content* in that *objects* and *tasks* for attention are primary in characterizing it. What makes a macro-grain pattern into a continuity of attention is its *intentional* properties. To that extent we might think of conscious attention as a highly embedded activity as well.

There are also clearly some interesting properties of the conscious mind within the domain of mental processing more generally that seem to have a fairly natural statement as a matter of informational encapsulation. There are obviously substantial restrictions on what information we can access. Outside conscious access lies the enormous amount of information coded into some fairly modular subsystems (like, perhaps, early vision, late motor control, and perhaps even parsing). How we speak in rhyme, how we make inductive inferences, how our desires get fixed, why we made one association rather than another, and even some of the more general strategies for problem-solving we might take—all are fairly opaque from our introspective queries. It's rightly tempting to see the isolation of conscious processing as the informational encapsulation of independent processes and their data—that is, to take conscious access as informational access, and to characterize the boundaries of the conscious as some boundary of informational opacity.

In any case, what might be contributed toward a naturalistic account of human consciousness by more information-processing oriented accounts is open. My point at present is just that it's not close to being the complete account. Both sides are needed: The conception of the activity as contentful and the conception of the underlying mechanisms and the implementations of that activity. We might then reasonably see two critical components that will be necessary parts in providing the naturalistic account we're dreaming of: Some kind of information-processing account is needed to account for something like the role of consciousness as distinctive within the domain of mental processes in general, while an approach from the perspective of the mind's embedding in the world is needed to capture intentional character of thought (and perception, and action). Perhaps taken together, these approaches may point us toward starting to (as Nagel puts it) "approach the gap between subjective and objective from another direction . . . [to] pursue a more objective understanding of the mental in its own right" [Nagel 1979, p. 178], and to meet the "challenge to form new concepts and devise a new method—an objective phenomenology not dependent on empathy or the imagination" [p. 179].

12.5. The Existential Turn

The existential turn in the phenomenological tradition involved a shift from taking intentional properties of thought as *immanent* (or directly present to reflection), as in Husserl, to seeing them as essentially determined by their relationship to the world, as in Heidegger and Merleau-Ponty. Existentialism thus "thrusts man back into the world" [Sartre 1957, p. 105]. At its heart is a breakdown of the Cartesian illusion of the mind as something that is independent of the surrounding world for its essence; a final collapse of the "fallacy of immanence" [Sartre 1957, p. 84].

By relocating the determinants of the content of thought and action into the shared world—the environment—the structure of intentionality becomes analyzable via the structure of the intentional objects, which are now the objects in the environment with which we all interact. As in the case of Simon's ant [Simon 1981b], whose complex path along the sand becomes understandable when we come to see it as the interaction of a simpler mechanism with a complex but accessible environmental structure, pushing more of the complexity of the structure of thought, perception, and action into the structure of the shared environment will reduce the impenetrable "internality" of subjectivity, and perhaps lend tractability to the problem of analyzing it.

The central catch-phrase of existentialism—"existence precedes essence"—is meant to capture the general theme that separates existential phenomenology from the earlier "pure" phenomenology of Husserl. The idea is that the existence (and perhaps, if you like, *embedding*) of thought in the real world is in some deep way logically prior to its essence or definition. Questions about the nature and content of thought must be asked while presupposing thought's embedding in the world. With the existential turn, "phenomenology is also a philosophy that puts essences back into existence, and does not expect to arrive at an understanding of man and the world from any starting point other than that of their 'facticity' " [Merleau-Ponty 1962, p. vii].

For Sartre and Merleau-Ponty, the essence of everything—including my self and its states of consciousness—is transcendent: it essentially goes beyond what is given in my consciousness, and depends for its essence on the real aspects of the world on which it is directed. This "plunges man back into the world" and opposes solipsism. It places us essentially in the world, with no special status; with nothing that makes the "I" essentially different from the ego of others or the world in general; it leaves "no sphere of immanence, no realm in which my consciousness is fully at home and secure against all risk of error" [Merleau-Ponty 1962, p. 376]. "The dualism of being and appearance is no longer entitled to any legal status within philosophy" [Sartre 1956, p. 4]; "Inside and outside are inseparable" [Merleau-Ponty 1962, p. 407].

This suggests a kind of *direct realism*. The appearances that reveal the world are "no longer interior nor exterior" [Sartre 1956, p. 4]. Appearances are not internal pictures, but (intentional) relations to the world; projections of the world, defined by their relationship to it. This is a rejection of reality as hidden and unreachable, as seen through the veil of perception. Appearances here are reality being given; they are projections of things in the world into consciousness, defined by the things themselves; not internally defined ideas from which objects in the world are constructions. We move away from "what Nietzsche called 'the illusion of worlds-behind-the-scene'"; we "no longer believe in the being-behind-the-appearance" [ibid.].

The rejection of the separability of mind from world has been the running theme of this book. The tactic has been mostly quite different, and the arguments have come mostly from the interpretation and meta-theory of the current sciences of the mind: Motivations for finding a place for such an account in part 1; considerations of tractability of task and the possibility of intelligent action given the overconstraints and underdeterminations faced in part 2; and support from contemporary accounts of language, problem-solving, and perception in part 3. But the undercurrent has been the same: Thought and action only make sense against the presupposition of a particular structured world; and to attempt analysis in isolation from that world is to welcome failure.

Thus for us too "existence precedes essence." The existence in the real world of my thoughts (and everything else) precedes their definition. This is an explicit rejection both of the Cartesian view of mind (where its essence is known before its real existence in the world) and of the positivist and Husserlian account of the meanings of words and thoughts (where what they mean and refer to is something in the essence of the symbol rather than in the world and in the real existent which is the intentional object of the thought). As it's clearly put by advocates of the "new" or "causal" account of meaning and reference: The reference of thoughts in the world is not secondary to their descriptive essence, but is primary, and in turn determines their intentional essence. As Sartre puts it in the introduction to *Being and Nothingness:* The "first procedure of a philosophy ought to be to expel things from consciousness and to reestablish its true connection with the world; to know that consciousness is a positional consciousness *of the world*" [Sartre 1956, p. 11]. Or in Merleau-Ponty's words: "The essential point is clearly to grasp the project towards the world that we are" [Merleau-Ponty 1962, p. 405].

REFERENCES

Agre, P., and D. Chapman. 1987. Pengi: An Implementation of a Theory of Activity. In *The Proceedings of the Sixth National Conference on Artificial Intelligence*, pp. 268–272. San Mateo, Calif.: Morgan Kaufmann.

Ballard, D. H. 1991. Animate Vision. *Artificial Intelligence* 48:57–86.

Barwise, J., and J. Perry. 1983. *Situations and Attitudes* Cambridge, Mass.: M.I.T. Press.

Block, N. 1978. Troubles with Functionalism. In N. Block, ed., *Readings in Philosophy of Psychology*, vol. 1, pp. 268–305. Cambridge, Mass.: Harvard University Press.

———. 1980. Are Absent Qualia Possible? *Philosophical Review*, 89:257–274.

Brandon, R. 1984. The Levels of Selection. In R. Brandon and R. Burian, eds., *Genes, Organisms, Populations: Controversies Over the Units of Selection*, pp. 133–141. Cambridge, Mass.: M.I.T. Press.

Burge, T. 1979a. Individualism and the Mental. In P. French, T. Uehling, and H. Wettstein, eds., *Midwest Studies in Philosophy*, pp. 73–121. Minneapolis: University of Minnesota Press.

———. 1979b. Sinning against Frege. *Philosophical Review* 88:398–432.

———. 1982. Other bodies. In A. Woodfield, ed., *Thought and Object*, pp. 97–120. Oxford: Clarendon Press.

———. 1986. Individualism and Psychology. *Philosophical Review* 95:3–45.

Chapman, D. 1990. On Choosing Domains for Agents. Manuscript.

Chomsky, N. 1965. *Aspects of the Theory of Syntax*. Cambridge, Mass.: M.I.T. Press.

———. 1972. *Language and Mind*. New York: Harcourt Brace Jovanovich.

———. 1980. Precis of Rules and Representations. *Behavioral and Brain Sciences* 3:1–15.

Churchland, P. 1979. *Scientific Realism and the Plasticity of the Mind*. Cambridge: Cambridge University Press.

———. 1984. *Matter and Consciousness*. Cambridge, Mass.: M.I.T. Press.

Cohen, P., and E. Feigenbaum. 1982. *The Handbook of Artificial Intelligence*, vol. 3. Los Altos, Calif.: Kaufmann.

Cooper, L., and R. Shepard. 1973. Chronometric Studies of the Rotation of Mental Images. In Chase, W. G., editor, *Visual Information Processing*, pp. 75–176. New York: Academic Press.

Cummins, R. 1983. *The Nature of Psychological Explanation*. Cambridge, Mass.: M.I.T. Press.

Dennett, D. 1978. Toward a Cognitive Theory of Consciousness. In *Brainstorms*, pp. 149–173. Montgomery, Vt.: Bradford Books.

Dennett, D. C. 1984. Cognitive Wheels: The Frame Problem of AI. In Hookway, ed., *Minds Machines, and Evolution*, pp. 129–151. Cambridge: Cambridge University Press.

———. 1990. Ways of Establishing Harmony. In E., Villanueva, ed., *Information, Semantics, and Epistemology*, pp. 18–27. Cambridge, Mass.: Basil Blackwell.

Dretske, F. 1990. Does Meaning Matter? *In* E., Villanueva, ed., *Information, Semantics and Epistemology*, pp. 5–17. Cambridge, Mass.: Basil Blackwell.

Dreyfus, H. 1979. *What Computers Can't Do*, second ed. New York: Harper and Row.

———. 1982. Introduction. *In* H. Dreyfus, ed., *Husserl Intentionality and Cognitive Science*, pp. 1–30. Cambridge, Mass.: M.I.T. Press.

Elster, J. 1983. *Explaining Technical Change*. Cambridge: Cambridge University Press.

Fitts, P., and M. Posner. 1967. *Human Performance*. Belmont, Calif.: Brooks/Cole.

Fodor, J. A. 1974. Special Sciences, or the Disunity of Science as a Working Hypothesis. *Synthese* 28:97–115.

———. 1980. Methodological Solipsism Considered as a Research Strategy in Cognitive Psychology. *Behavioral and Brain Sciences* 3:63–73.

———. 1983. *The Modularity of Mind: An Essay on Faculty Psychology*. Cambridge, Mass.: M.I.T. Press.

———. 1987a. Modules, Frames, Fridgeons, Sleeping Dogs, and the Music of the Spheres. *In* Z. Pylyshyn, ed., *The Robot's Dilemma: The Frame Problem in Artificial Intelligence*, pp. 139–149. Norwood, N.J.: Ablex.

———. 1987b. *Psychosemantics: The Problem of Meaning in the Philosophy of Mind*. Cambridge, Mass.: M.I.T. Press.

Fodor, J. A., and Z. Pylyshyn. 1981. How Direct is Visual Perception? Some Reflections on Gibson's Ecological Approach. *Cognition* 9:139–196.

———. 1988. Connectionism and Cognitive Architecture. *Cognition* 28:3–71.

Frege, G. 1980. On Sense and Meaning. *In* P. Geach and M. Black, eds., *Translations from the Philosophical Writings of Gottlob Frege*, third ed., pp. 56–78. Totowa, N.J.: Rowman and Littlefield.

Gardner, H. 1984. *The Mind's New Science: A History of the Cognitive Revolution*. New York: Basic Books.

Gibson, J. J. 1986. *The Ecological Approach to Visual Perception* Hillsdale, N.J.: Lawrence Erlbaum Associates.

Gilovich, T., R. Vallone, and A. Tversky. 1985. The Hot Hand in Basketball: On the Misperception of Random Sequences. *Cognitive Psychology* 17:295–314.

Goodman, N. 1954. *Fact, Fiction, and Forecast.* Cambridge, Mass.: Harvard University Press.

Gould, S. J. 1984. Caring Groups and Selfish Genes. *In* Sober, E., editor, *Conceptual Issues in Evolutionary Biology,* pp. 119–124. Cambridge, Mass.: M.I.T. Press.

Gould, S. J., and R. Lewontin, 1984. The Spandrels of San Marcos and the Panglossian Paradigm: A Critique of the Adaptationist Programme. In E. Sober, ed., *Conceptual Issues in Evolutionary Biology,* pp. 252–270. Cambridge, Mass.: M.I.T. Press.

Hacking, I. 1983. *Representing and Intervening: Introductory Topics in the Philosophy of Natural Science.* Cambridge: Cambridge University Press.

Hammond, K. J. 1990. Learning and Enforcement: Stabilizing Environments to Facilitate Activity. *In* B. Porter and R. Mooney, eds. *The Proceedings of the Seventh International Conference on Machine Learning,* pp. 204–210. San Mateo, Calif.: Morgan Kaufmann.

———. 1991. Opportunistic Memory. Manuscript.

Hanks, S. 1990. Controlling Inference in a Planning Systems: Who, What, When, Why, and How. Technical Report 90-04-01, University of Washington Department of Computer Science and Engineering.

Hardin, C. L. 1988. *Color for Philosophers.* Indianapolis, Ind.: Hackett.

Haugeland, J. 1980. Semantic Engines: An Introduction to Mind Design. In Haugeland, J., editor, Mind Design, pp. 1–34. Cambridge, Mass.: M.I.T. Press.

———. 1982. Weak Supervenience. *American Philosophical Quarterly* 19:93–103.

Horswill, I., and R. A. Brooks. 1989. Situated Vision in a Dynamic World: Chasing Objects. *In* N. Sridharan, ed., *Proceedings of the Eleventh International Joint Conference on Artificial Intelligence,* pp. 796–800. San Mateo, Calif.: Morgan Kaufmann.

Husserl, E. 1962. *Ideas: General Introduction to Pure Phenomenology.* New York: Collier Books.

———. 1964. *The Idea of Phenomenology.* The Hauge: Martinus Nijhoff.

Jackendoff, R. 1987. *Consciousness and the Computational Mind.* Cambridge, Mass.: M.I.T. Press.

Johnson-Laird, P. N. 1983. A Computational Analysis of Consciousness. *Cognition and Brain Theory* 6:500–508.

Joos, M. 1948. Acoustic Phonetics. *Language* (supplement), 24:1–136.

Kaplan, D. 1989. Demonstratives. In J. Almog, J. Perry, and H. Wettstein, eds., *Themes from Kaplan,* pages 481–614. New York: Oxford University Press.

Kirsh, D. 1991. Today the Earwig, Tomorrow Man? *Artificial Intelligence* 47:161–184.

Kitcher, P. 1985. Darwin's Achievement. *In* N. Rescher, ed., *Reason and Rationality in Natural Science*, pp. 127–189. Lanham, Md.: University Press of America.

Kripke, S. 1980. *Naming and Necessity.* Cambridge, Mass.: Harvard University Press.

Leeper, R. 1935. The Role of Motivation in Learning: A Study of the Phenomenon of Differential Motivational Control of the Utilization of Habits. *Journal of Genetic Psychology* 46:41–75.

Leibniz, G. W. 1962. The Monadology: *In* G. Montgomery, trans., *Leibniz: Basic Writings*, pp. 257–272. La Salle, Ill.: Open Court.

Lewontin, R. C. 1970. The Units of Selection. *Annual Review of Ecology and Systematics* 1:1–18.

Liberman, A., F. Cooper, D. Shankweiler, and M. Studdert-Kennedy. 1967. Perception of the Speech Code. *Psychological Review* 74:431–461.

Lycan, W. 1980. The functionalist Reply (Ohio State). *Behavioral and Brain Sciences* 3:434–435.

———. 1988. *Consciousness.* Cambridge, Mass.: M.I.T. Press.

Marr, D. 1982. *Vision.* San Francisco, Calif.: Freeman.

Massaro, D. W., and M. M. Cohen. 1983. Evaluation and Integration of Visual and Auditory Information in Speech Perception. *Journal of Experimental Psychology: Human Perception and Performance* 9:753–771.

Mayr, E. 1984. The Unity of the Genotype. *In* R. Brandon and R. Burian, eds., *Genes, Organisms, Populations: Controversies Over the Units of Selection.* Cambridge Mass.: M.I.T. Press.

McClamrock, R. 1989. Holism without Tears: Local and Global Effects in Cognitive Processes. *Philosophy of Science* 56:258–274.

———. 1991. Marr's Three Levels: A Re-evaluation. *Minds and machines* 1:185–196.

———. 1993. Functional Analysis and etiology. *Erkenntnis* 38(2):249–260.

McDermott, D. 1987. We've Been Framed: Or, Why AI is Innocent of the Frame Problem. *In* Z. Pylyshyn, ed., *The Robot's Dilemma*, pp. 113–122. Norwood, N.J. Ablex.

McGurk, H, and MacDonald, J. 1976. Hearing Lips and Seeing Voices. *Nature* 264:746–748.

Merleau-Ponty, M. 1962. *Phenomenology of Perception.* London: Routledge and Kegan Paul.

Meyer, D., and R. Schvanevedlt. 1971. Facilitation in Recognizing Pairs of Words: Evidence of a Dependence between Retrieval Operations. *Journal of Experimental Psychology: General* 90:227–234.

Miller, J. L. 1981. Effects of Speaking Rate on Segmental Distinctions. *In* P. Eimas and J. Miller, eds., *Perspectives on the Study of Speech*, pp. 39–74. Hillsdale, N.J.: Lawrence Erlbaum Associates.

Miller, J. L. 1981. Effects of Speaking Rate on Segmental Distinctions. *In* P. Eimas and J. Miller, eds., *Perspectives on the Study of Speech*, pp. 39–74. Hillsdale, N.J.: Lawrence Erlbaum Associates.

Nagel T. 1979. What Is It Like to Be a Bat? *In Mortal Questions*, pp. 165–180. Cambridge: Cambridge University Press.

Neisser, U. 1976. *Cognition and Reality: Principles and Implications of Cognitive Psychology*. San Francisco; Calif.: Freeman.

Nusbaum, H., and J. DeGroot. 1991. The Role of Syllables in Speech Perception. In M. S. Ziolkowski, M. Noske, and K. Deaton, editors, *Papers from the Parasession on the Syllable in Phonetics and Phonology*. Chicago: University of Chicago Press.

Oatley, K. 1980. *Perception and Representation*. New York: Free Press.

Olson, T. J., and D. J. Coombs. 1990. Real-time Vergence Control for Binocular Robots. Technical Report 348, University of Rochester, Rochester, N.Y.

Perry, J. 1977. Frege on Demonstratives. *The Philosophical Review* 86:474–497.

Putnam, H. 1963. Brains and Behavior. In R. Butler, ed., *Analytical Philosophy: Second Series*, pp. 325–341. Oxford: Basil Blackwell and Mott.

———. 1970. Is Semantics Possible? *In* H. Kiefer and M. Munitz, eds., *Language, Belief, and Metaphysics*, pp. 50–63. New York: State University of New York Press.

———. 1973. Reductionism and the Nature of Psychology. *Cognition* 2:131–146.

———. 1975. The Meaning of "Meaning." In *Mind, Language, and Reality: Philosophical Papers: Vol. 2*, pp. 215–271. Cambridge: Cambridge University Press.

———. 1981. *Reason, Truth and History*. New York: Cambridge University Press.

———. 1984. Computational Psychology and Interpretation Theory: In *Realism and Reason: Philosophical Papers, Vol. 2*. Cambridge: Cambridge University Press.

Pylyshyn, Z. W. 1984. *Computation and Cognition: Toward a Foundation for Cognitive Science*. Cambridge Mass.: M.I.T. Press.

Quine, W. 1953. Two Dogmas of Empiricism. In *From a Logical Point of View*, pp. 20–46. Cambridge Mass.: Harvard University Press.

Rosch, E., and C. Mervis. 1975. Family Resemblances: Studies in the Internal Structure of Categories. *Cognitive Psychology* 7:573–605.

Russell, S. 1989. Execution Architectures and Compilation. *In* N. Sridharan, ed., *Proceedings of the Twelfth International Joint Conference on Artificial Intelligence*, vol. 89, pp. 15–20. San Mateo, Calif.: Morgan Kaufmann.

Russell, S., and E. Wefald. 1989. On Optimal Game-Tree Search Using Rational Meta-reasoning. *In* N. Sridharan, ed., *Proceedings of the*

Eleventh International Joint Conference on Artificial Intelligence, vol. 89, pp. 334–340. San Mateo, Calif.: Morgan Kaufmann.

Salmon, W. 1984. *Scientific Explanation and the Causal Structure of the World.* Princeton, N.J.: Princeton University Press.

Sartre, J.-P. 1956. *Being and Nothingness.* New York: Washington Square Press.

———. 1957. *The Transcendence of the Ego: An Existentialist Theory of Consciousness.* New York: Noonday Press.

Schiffer, S. R. 1987. *Remnants of Meaning.* Cambridge, Mass.: M.I.T. Press.

Searle, J. 1980. Minds, Brains, and Programs. *Behavioral and Brain Sciences* 3:417–424.

———. 1983. *Intentionality.* Cambridge: Cambridge University Press.

Shapiro, S. 1987. *The Encyclopedia of Artificial Intelligence.* New York: Wiley.

Shaw, R., and J. Bransford, 1977. Introduction: Psychological Approaches to the Problem of Knowledge. *In* R. Shaw and J. Bransford, eds., *Perceiving, Acting, and Knowing: Toward an Ecological Psychology*, pp. 1–39. Hillsdale, N.J.: Lawrence Erlbaum Associates.

Simon, H. 1957. *Administrative Behavior*, third ed. New York: Macmillan.

———. 1981a. Economic Rationality. In *The Sciences of the Artificial*, pp. 30–61. Cambridge, Mass.: M.I.T. Press.

———. 1981b. The Psychology of Thinking: Embedding Artifice in Nature. In *The Sciences of the Artificial*, pp. 62–98. Cambridge, Mass.: M.I.T. Press.

Smith, D. W., and R. McIntyre. 1982. *Husserl and Intentionality: A Study of Mind, Meaning, and Language.* Dordrecht: Reidel.

Sober, E. 1984a. Holism, Individualism, and the Units of Selection. *In* E. Sober, ed., *Conceptual Issues in Evolutionary Biology*, pp. 184–209. Cambridge, Mass.: M.I.T. Press.

———. 1984b. *The Nature of Selection*, Cambridge, Mass.: M.I.T. Press.

———. 1988. *Reconstructing the Past.* Cambridge, Mass.: M.I.T. Press.

Sober, E., and R. C. Lewontin, 1984. Artifact, Cause, and Genic Selection. *In* E. Sober, ed., *Conceptual Issues in Evolutionary Biology*, pages 210–232. Cambridge, Mass.: M.I.T. Press.

Stanovich, K. E., and R. F. West. 1981. The Effect of Sentence Context on Ongoing Word Recognition: Tests of a Two-Process Theory. *Journal of Experimental Psychology: Human Perception and Performance* 7:658–672.

Swain, M. J., and D. H. Ballard. 1992. Low Resolution Cues for Guiding Saccadic Eye Movements. In *Proceedings of IEEE Conference on Computer Vision and Pattern Recognition.*

Thurow, L. C. 1983. Rebuilding the Foundations of Economics: Catching the Trade Winds. *In* L. Thurow, ed. *Dangerous Currents: The State of Economics*, pp. 216–237. New York: Vintage Books.

Todd, J. T. 1983. Perception of Gait. *Journal of Experimental Psychology: Human Perception and Performance* 9:31–42.

Tversky, A, and D. Kahneman. 1974. Judgments of and by Representativeness. *Science* 185:1124–1131.

———. 1982. Evidential Impact of Base Rates. In D. Kahneman, P. Slovic, and A. Tversky, eds., *Judgment under uncertainty: Heuristics and Biases*, pp. 153–160. Cambridge: Cambridge University Press.

Wilson, P. 1991. Pointer Swizzling at Page Fault Time: Efficiently Supporting Huge Address Spaces on Standard Hardware. *Computer Architecture News* 19:6–13.

Wimsatt, W. C. 1984. Reductionistic Research Strategies and their Biases in the Units of Selection Controversy. *In* E. Sober, ed., *Conceptual Issues in Evolutionary Biology*, pp. 184–209. Cambridge, Mass.: M.I.T. Press.

———. 1986. Heuristics and the Study of Human Behavior. *In* D. Fiske and R. Shweder, eds. *Metatheory in Social Science: Pluralisms and Subjectivities*, pp. 293–314. Chicago: University of Chicago Press.

Winston, P. 1975. *The Psychology of Computer Vision*. New York: McGraw-Hill.

Witkin, A. P., and J. M. Tenenbaum. On the Role of Structure in Vision. In A. Witkin and J. Tenenbaum, eds., *Human and Machine Vision*, pp. 481–543. New York. Academic Press.

Yarbus, A. L. 1967. *Eye Movements and Vision*. New York: Plenum.

INDEX